STRUCTURED FINANCE

A Guide to the Principles of Asset Securitization

Second Edition

STRUCTURED FINANCE

A Guide to the Principles of Asset Securitization

Second Edition

Steven L. Schwarcz

Fourth Printing

A1-1418

Practising Law Institute

This publication is designed to provide accurate and authoritative information in regard to the subject matter covered. It is sold with the understanding that the publisher is not engaged in rendering legal, accounting, or other professional service. If legal advice or other expert assistance is required, the services of a competent professional person should be sought.

— From Declaration of Principles jointly adopted by Committee of American Bar Association and Committee of Publishers and Associations

Published by
Practising Law Institute
810 Seventh Avenue
New York, N.Y. 10019

Copyright © 1990, 1993 by Practising Law Institute, All rights reserved. Printed in the United States of America. No part of this publication may be reproduced, stored in a retrieval system, or transmitted in any form by any means, electronic, mechanical, photocopying, recording, or otherwise, without prior written permission of Practising Law Institute.

Library of Congress Catalog Card Number: 93-083776
ISBN: 0-87224-056-8

The author dedicates this monograph to his wonderful wife, Susan, and to their children, Daniel and Rebekah (who provide challenges that sometime even exceed those described in this monograph).

About the Author

STEVEN L. SCHWARCZ is a partner of Kaye, Scholer, Fierman, Hays & Handler and Chairman of its Structured Finance Practice Group; Visiting Lecturer at the Yale Law School, teaching the course in Structuring Commercial Transactions; Lecturer in Law at Columbia Law School, teaching the course in Structuring Commercial Transactions; and Adjunct Professor of Law at Benjamin N. Cardozo School of Law, Yeshiva University, teaching the Advanced Seminar in Bankruptcy and Corporate Reorganization.

Table of Contents

Acknowledgments ix
Foreword to the Second Edition xi
Foreword to the First Edition xiii

Introduction 1
History 3
Defining the Source of Payment 5
    Nature of the Obligors and the Originator 5
    Nature of the Receivables. 7
    Financial Guarantees and Credit Supports 13
Separating the Source of Payment from the Originator 16
    Making the SPV "Bankruptcy-Remote" 16
        Protecting the SPV from Voluntary and
            Involuntary Bankruptcy 16
        Protecting the SPV from Substantive Consolidation 24
        Protecting the SPV from Governmental Claims. 26
    Creating a "True Sale" of the Receivables 28
        Recourse 31
        Retained Rights and Right to Surplus 32
        Pricing Mechanism 32
        Administration and Collection of Accounts 33
        Additional Factors 34
    Protecting Against the Fraudulent Conveyance Risk 35
    Additional Steps Required Under the UCC
        to Protect the Transfer 37
        Perfecting the Transfer. 37
        Commingling 40

Debtor-in-Possession (DIP) Securitization.	40
Tax Issues.	45
Taxation of the Originator	46
Taxation of the SPV.	49
Taxation of the Investors	52
Regulatory Requirements.	53
Investment Company Act of 1940	54
Securities Act of 1933 and Securities Exchange Act of 1934.	61
Other Regulatory Requirements.	66
Risk-Based Capital Requirements	68
The Guidelines Generally.	69
The Effect of the Guidelines on an Originator of Receivables.	71
The Effect of the Guidelines on Providers of Credit Enhancement or Liquidity	73
The Effect of the Guidelines on Investors in Structured Finance Transactions	76
Conclusion.	76
Tables of Authorities.	77
Index	87

Acknowledgments

The author wishes to thank, for their helpful and insightful comments, his partners, especially Gary Apfel, T. Brent Costello, Herbert S. Edelman, Leslie H. Loffman, Eric P. Marcus, Renée E. Ring, Willys H. Schneider, Arthur Steinberg, and Peter H. Weil; Myron Glucksman, Mark P. Trager, and Frank J. Cavallo, Vice Presidents of Citicorp Securities Markets, Inc.; Fernando Guerrero, Vice President of Chemical Securities Inc.; and Frank W. Hamilton III.

The author further thanks his colleagues, Robert A. Villani and Terry D. Novetsky, for invaluable assistance in the preparation of the second edition of this monograph.

This monograph is a revised and expanded version of an article originally published in the *Cardozo Law Review*.

Foreword to the Second Edition

Schwarcz's *Structured Finance* has proved to be an indispensable guide. It is accessible to bankers and other business people, practicing lawyers, and legal scholars alike. Although its lucid but concise explanations easily can be understood by a novice, its in-depth treatment is invaluable for the expert as well.

Clarity remains one of the principal strengths of this second edition. Significantly, the book informs the legal specialist about the business and financial underpinnings of structured finance while illuminating the legal issues for the business person. And Mr. Schwarcz has accomplished this feat without compromising the book's sophistication. He has provided a view of the subject from the scholarly as well as the practical perspectives. (Not surprisingly, Mr. Schwarcz teaches courses on structured finance at the Yale Law School and the Columbia Law School.)

Happily, the substance of Peter Weil's insightful Foreword to the first edition (which I commend to the readers) applies equally well to the second edition; it is necessary here only to highlight some of the new material included in the second edition.

Structured Finance (Second Edition) describes significant recent market and legal developments, such as securitizations involving originators whose securities are below investment grade and originators who are debtors in possession under Chapter 11 of the Bankruptcy Code, and important new changes in the application of the securities laws to structured finance. The new edition also explains and draws lessons from the recent Days Inn bankruptcy and the impact of that bankruptcy on the Days Inn franchise fee securitization facility. Those lessons include the means of structuring a securitization "poison pill" and the manner in which the Days Inn special-purpose vehicle might have been structured so as to avoid its bankruptcy filing. (The monograph emphasizes throughout the importance of bankruptcy issues in properly structuring a transaction.) The second edition also addresses other new developments, such as the duties of directors who serve on the board of a special-purpose vehicle, master trusts, compliance with risk-based capital requirements, and the creation of a "FINCO," or "two-tiered," structure.

In a word, *Structured Finance* is "must" reading for anyone involved or seriously interested in finance.

CHARLES W. MOONEY, JR.
Professor of Law
The Law School
University of Pennsylvania

Foreword to the First Edition

Business finance has been and is a dynamic field in which the development of the law has assisted the business world in achieving its goals. Those goals include creating flexible means to accelerate the cash cycle of different businesses, using various business assets as the basis for the acceleration, and creating structures that will give a high enough level of comfort to the financing sources so that the cash will be made available.

The idea of collateral security is an ancient one in general.[1] Its refinement has been an evolutionary process. Rumors aside, tangible property that could be taken into the financer's possession was the first, most obvious concept. Shylock's pound of flesh was a bizarre form of security, which even the Uniform Commercial Code has declined to recognize. Between these two extremes, the financial world has gradually broadened the spectrum of assets that it would accept as collateral.

Accounts receivable have been subject to various forms of assignment, voluntary and involuntary, for a long time, although the legal mechanisms to implement and perfect those assignments were (except in the case of attaching judgment creditors) very variable, and not always structured to give the lender the absolute assurance of protection that it would want.

The concept of the sale of accounts receivable without recourse, or "factoring," did not arise until the 19th century, when the lack of rapid communications forced salesmen in the field to take responsi-

---

1. It has even been rumored that, as far back as the Dark Ages, a customer who failed to pay his exorcist would be repossessed.

xiii

bility for the credit of the customers to whom they were selling the goods of the manufacturer they were representing. The credit risk function eventually split off from the sales function, and factoring was born.

Again, as an evolutionary process, other forms of receivable sales were developed. The use of the sale format to achieve off-balance-sheet financing was offered by major banks to substantial corporations which would not be caught dead signing a factoring contract. At the same time, the transactions got more complex and involved more and more aspects of other fields of law, specifically tax, bankruptcy, and securities law. The business, finance, and legal people continued to exercise their imaginations.

Which brings us to structured finance and asset securitization.

Not only do these techniques represent a refinement of everything that went before them, they expand the scope of business finance in terms of flexibility as to (1) terms and structure (for example, whether the transaction is a sale or loan for accounting, tax, or bankruptcy purposes; the criteria differ), (2) assets that can be financed (not only accounts receivable but future, and even contingent, cash flows), and (3) the sources of the cash to do the transaction (whether commercial paper, longer-term notes, senior or junior participations, or others).

Given the many permutations and combinations that are possible for a particular transaction, in concert with the multiplicity of legal disciplines that are involved in each transaction, it is remarkable to find that that subject can be presented comprehensively as well as comprehensibly in a monograph as concise as this one. While brevity may be the soul of wit, it is also the cornerstone of good communication. Nevertheless, all significant issues affecting a structured finance and asset securitization transaction are discussed in sufficient detail so that the reader, after absorbing all that the author has to say, will have a thorough understanding of the elements and complexities of structured finance and asset securitization. While avoiding lengthy citations, the author provides ample authorities to point the reader in the proper direction to research such refinements as may not be covered here. The text is at the same time clear, compact, and meaty; the thoughtful reader will enjoy the experience.

It is well established that the briefer the presentation to be made, the more the author must know about his subject. The author of this monograph is uniquely equipped for the task. Not only is Mr. Schwarcz one of the two or three practitioners who are recognized by the financial community as the leading experts in the field of structured finance and asset securitization, he is (in what passes for his spare time) a law school professor in two of the core areas on which structured finance and asset securitization are based. He is also the author of a sizable list of published articles on those and related topics. We are fortunate that he has decided to share his knowledge and expertise with us in a unified and thorough presentation.

PETER H. WEIL
Kaye, Scholer, Fierman, Hays & Handler

Introduction

Traditionally a company will raise money by issuing securities that represent equity in the company or, in the case of debt securities, entitle the holders to claims for repayment. Sometimes payment of those claims is secured by a lien on certain of the company's properties. In each case the security holder looks primarily to the company for repayment. If the company becomes financially troubled, or bankrupt, payment of the securities may be jeopardized, or at least delayed.

Structured finance can change the security holder's dependence on the company for payment, by separating the source of payment from the company itself. In a typical structured financing, a company that seeks to raise cash may sell certain of its assets to a special-purpose vehicle or trust (hereinafter called the SPV) that is organized in such a way that the likelihood of its bankruptcy is remote. The "sale" can be accomplished in a manner that to a certain extent removes those assets from the estate of the selling company even in the event of its bankruptcy. The result is that the assets are no longer owned by the selling company, but by the bankruptcy-remote vehicle or trust. The assets themselves are typically payment obligations, such as accounts or other amounts receivable, owing to the company from third parties. (In this monograph, those payment obligations generically are referred to as "receivables.")

The SPV, and not the selling company, will issue securities to raise cash. Those securities are intended to be payable from collections on the receivables purchased by the SPV. A potential buyer of the securities therefore looks to the cash flow from the purchased receivables, and not necessarily to the credit of the selling company, for repayment.

The separation of the selling company (hereinafter called the originator, because it usually originates the receivables) from the receivables themselves can enable the originator to raise funds at less

Structured Finance

expense, through securities issued by the SPV, than if it raised funds through securities it issued directly. (For example, the securities issued by the SPV, depending upon the structure of the transaction, may have a higher investment rating than securities issued directly by the originator and, therefore, would bear a lower interest rate than the originator might be able to obtain on its own securities, bank lines of credit, or secured borrowings.) In addition, as illustrated in the table below, the cash that is raised usually will not require an offsetting liability to be shown on the originator's balance sheet; from the standpoint of the originator, the cash represents proceeds of the sale of receivables to the SPV.

Balance Sheet Impact of Securitizing Assets of XYZ Company

Assets	Liabilities	Equity	Ratio
Receivables $100	Debt $100	Equity $100	Debt/Equity=1/1
Equipment $100			

1. If *XYZ* Company borrows $100, secured by its receivables, its ratio of debt to equity worsens (or, if used to pay down debt, remains the same):

Assets	Liabilities	Equity	Ratio Worse
Cash $100	Debt $200	Equity $100	Debt/Equity=2/1
Receivables $100			
Equipment $100			

2. But if *XYZ* Company sells $100 of its receivables:

Assets	Liabilities	Equity	Ratio Unchanged
Cash $100	Debt $100	Equity $100	Debt/Equity=1/1
Equipment $100			

3. And if *XYZ* Company then uses $90, for example, of the cash to pay off debt, its ratio of debt to equity dramatically improves:

Assets	Liabilities	Equity	Ratio Improved
Cash $10	Debt $10	Equity $100	Debt/Equity=1/10
Equipment $100			

The table assumes the receivables are sold at face value.

Asset Securitization

If the originator is a bank or similar financial institution that is required to maintain risk-based capital under the capital-adequacy guidelines,[1] securitization could also permit the originator to sell assets (e.g., loans reflected as assets on a bank's financial statements) for which it would otherwise be required to maintain capital. That reduces the bank's effective cost of funds.

Further, an originator may be restricted by its indenture covenants from incurring or securing debt beyond a specified level. A structured financing may enable the originator to raise cash in compliance with such covenants, because the originator may be selling assets and not incurring or securing debt. (Whether a structured financing would violate particular covenants requires a case-by-case inquiry.)

History

The first structured financings to be identified as such took place in the early 1970s with the securitization of pools of mortgages. Initially, mortgages were originated by savings and loan associations, which depended heavily on core deposit flows for funds to finance local housing demand. When the housing credit market collapsed during the Depression, Congress reacted by passing the National Housing Act of 1934, intended in part to create a secondary market in mortgages. To that end, the Federal National Mortgage Association was established in 1938 to provide liquidity for mortgage investment by purchasing mortgages when funds are in short supply and selling mortgages when funds are plentiful. As the nation's demand for housing increased after World War II, a capital shortage developed, and alternative capital streams were needed to finance the growing housing industry. In 1957, the Federal Home Loan Bank Board created a credit reserve system for savings and loan associa-

---

1. *See Capital Adequacy Guidelines for Bank Holding Companies and State Member Banks: Leverage Measure,* 12 C.F.R. pt. 225, app. B (1992), and discussion *infra* under "Bank Capital Requirements."

tions by permitting the purchase and sale of participations in interests in mortgage loans.

The first structured financing came in 1970 when the newly created Government National Mortgage Association began publicly trading "pass-through" securities. In a mortgage pass-through security, the investor purchases a fractional undivided interest in a pool of mortgage loans, and is entitled to share in the interest income and principal payments generated by the underlying mortgages. Mortgage lenders originate pools of mortgages with similar characteristics as to quality, term, and interest rate. The pool is placed in a trust. Then, through either a government agency, a private conduit, or direct placement, certificates of ownership are sold to investors. Income from the mortgage pool passes through to the investors.

In recent years, many different types of assets have been the subject of securitization.[2] When the securities issued by the SPV are publicly issued, and rating agencies — such as Standard & Poor's and Moody's — rate those securities, the assets purchased by the SPV tend to be payment streams that have proven histories of past payment and predictable expectations of future payment. Examples would include pools of residential and commercial mortgage loans, trade receivables, automobile loans, and credit card receivables.

On the other hand, when the securities are privately placed, the investors themselves can do the analysis needed to become comfortable with nonstandard payment streams. For example, recent private placement transactions have included payment streams consisting of franchise fees, equipment leases, subrogation claims, junk bonds, health care receivables, future media revenues, and even utility surcharges.

---

2. Securitization has also recently become a significant form of financing in foreign markets. *See, e.g.*, ASSET SECURITIZATION, INTERNATIONAL FINANCIAL AND LEGAL PERSPECTIVES (Norton & Spellman eds., 1991); *Securitization: Europe's Other Challenge*, CORP. FIN., Nov. 1989.

Asset Securitization

Defining the Source of Payment

As can be seen, the common thread is that the receivables purchased consist of a payment stream as to which there is a reasonable predictability of payment. Collections on the receivables would be applied to pay principal and interest on the securities issued by the SPV.

Nature of the Obligors and the Originator

Predictability of payment is affected by the nature and identity of both the obligors on the receivables and the originator, and also by the nature of the receivables themselves. With respect to the obligors, there are two risks: delay in payment (sometimes referred to as "slow pay") and default in payment (sometimes referred to as "no pay").

The slow-pay risk is that the obligors on the receivables may delay in making their payments. A holder of securities issued by the SPV would not be pleased to learn that its monthly or quarterly interest payment was not made because an obligor delayed its payment. For that reason, the number of obligors on the receivables should be large enough to maintain statistical assurance that even if a reasonably expected number of obligors delay in making their payments the securities issued by the SPV will be paid on time. Alternatively, payment streams that are uncertain as to precise timing of collections may be able to be securitized if a loan commitment or similar facility (referred to as a "liquidity facility") is provided to advance funds to the SPV to pay debt service if collections are temporarily delayed. Notwithstanding that security holders obtain comfort as to timing of collection, however, a liquidity facility does not necessarily protect the security holders in the case of larger-than-anticipated defaults.

The no-pay risk is that the obligors on the receivables may default in making their payments. That risk in turn depends on several factors. An obvious factor is the financial ability of the obligors to pay the receivables; an obligor might not pay because it is bankrupt or

5

Structured Finance

otherwise having financial problems. An obligor also may have a defense to payment.[3] Therefore, the number of obligors on the receivables again must be large enough so that the risk of default can be statistically determined.

There are, however, certain factors that can impair the validity of a statistical analysis. It may be that a relatively small number of the obligors (counting, for that purpose, affiliated obligors as a single obligor, because default by any given obligor may signify financial trouble for its affiliates) account for a disproportionately large amount of payments under the receivables. Default by those obligors might impair the ability of the security holders to be repaid. That risk of high concentrations of payments in a relatively small number of obligors is called, naturally enough, the obligor-concentration risk.

The default risk, therefore, can be managed by the SPV's buying receivables having a statistically large number of obligors, and by analyzing the obligor concentrations. The financial ability of the obligors to pay, and the possibility that the obligors may be able to assert defenses to payment, also would be considered. The default risk then may be addressed by the originator's adjusting the purchase and sale price of the receivables to take into account anticipated defaults.

There are various ways to compute the purchase and sale price. The most straightforward is to discount the outstanding balance of the receivables to be purchased, taking into account anticipated defaults and delays in collection. If the discount is too small, however, the SPV's security holders could suffer a loss. But if the discount is too large, the originator would be underpricing its receivables. Sometimes the discount is intentionally small, but the SPV has a degree of additional recourse (a loss reserve) against the originator or against additional receivables. Other times the discount is intentionally large (sometimes referred to as overcollateralization), but the originator retains a right to certain excess collections if the actual defaults do not turn out to justify the large discount (payment of a

---

3. The rights of a transferee of receivables may be subject to obligor defenses. *See* U.C.C. § 9-318(1).

"holdback"). These are merely examples. The method of pricing that is selected will depend on business and credit considerations that are beyond the scope of this monograph. It should be noted, however, that the more straightforward the method of pricing, and the more the SPV bears the risks and benefits of ownership, the more likely it is that the sale of receivables will be considered a true sale for bankruptcy purposes. See the discussion under "Creating a 'True Sale' of the Receivables."

Predictability of payment also depends on the nature and identity of the originator. A financially troubled originator is more likely to go bankrupt, thereby raising the question whether the transfer of its receivables is a sale for bankruptcy purposes. If a court holds the transfer not to be a sale for that purpose, the ability of the SPV to receive collections on the receivables will be delayed and may be seriously impaired.

Nature of the Receivables

Finally, predictability of payment may depend on the nature of the receivables themselves. For example, if the receivables constitute obligations owing for goods sold or services rendered (standard trade receivables), there are few defenses to payment. Perhaps some of the goods sold may turn out to be defective, or some of the obligors may turn out to be minors. In general a buyer of the receivables can anticipate the delinquency and default risks based on past collection patterns.

That type of predictability may not be obtained if the receivables represent payment for future performance obligations of the originator. An example is franchise fees. These are amounts payable from obligors, called franchisees, to a franchisor (the originator) in return for the license to run a business using a special trade name or trademark and selling designated products or services.[4]

---

4. *See, e.g.*, BLACK'S LAW DICTIONARY 592 (5th ed. 1979) (definition of franchise). It is typical for franchise agreements, and indeed many other types of long-term contracts, to contain prohibitions on assignment. That should not, however, prohibit

Structured Finance

Franchise fees may not be payment obligations at all, but merely expectations of payment. The fees may be calculated, for example, by a percentage (or other formula) of the franchisee's monthly or other periodic revenues or profits. If there are no revenues or profits, no franchise fee is payable. Also, if the franchisor (originator) fails to perform the contractually agreed upon franchise services, the franchisee may have a legal defense against payment of franchise fees.

In addition, in the case of a bankruptcy of the originator, the originator (or its trustee in bankruptcy) may have the right, under section 365 of the Bankruptcy Code, to reject, or terminate, the franchise agreement as an executory contract. An executory contract is any contract on which substantial performance remains due on both sides such that breach by one party of its performance obligations would excuse the other side's obligation to perform.[5] A franchise agreement would appear to be that type of contract.[6] Accordingly, an originator that becomes the subject of a bankruptcy case may be able to terminate the contract if it has business reasons to do so.[7] A possible solution to the executory contract risk would be to assign the franchise

---

the assignment of the right to payments made thereunder. Even if the contract purports to prohibit the assignment of rights thereunder, such a prohibition may be ineffective as a matter of law. *See* U.C.C. § 9-318(4) & cmt. 4.

5. *See* H.R. REP. NO. 595, 95th Cong., 1st Sess. 347 (1977); *see also In re* Streets & Beard Farm Partnership, 882 F.2d 233 (7th Cir. 1989); *In re* Grayson-Robinson Stores, Inc., 321 F.2d 500 (2d Cir. 1963); 2 WILLIAM MILLER COLLIER, COLLIER ON BANKRUPTCY §§ 365-01, -02, -05, -06, -08 (15th ed. 1989).
6. *See, e.g.*, Rosenthal Paper Co. v. National Folding Box & Paper Co., 123 N.E. 766 (N.Y. 1919); Isquith v. New York State Thruway Auth., 215 N.Y.S.2d 393, 397 (Ct. Cl. 1961) (thruway toll ticket as executory contract); Gerry v. Johnston, 378 P.2d 198 (Idaho 1919). Many contracts have been held to be executory even when the performance obligation has not been obvious. For example, a lease has been held to be an executory contract because of the lessor's obligation not to interfere with the lessee's right of quiet enjoyment. *See, e.g., In re* O.P.M. Leasing Servs., Inc., 23 B.R. 104, 117 (Bankr. S.D.N.Y. 1982).
7. For example, the franchisor may be unable to provide the products or perform the training or other services, if any, required under the franchise contract; or the originator may wish to terminate the existing franchise and enter into a new franchise contract (not subject to the structured financing) with the same franchisee.

Asset Securitization

agreements, if assignment is permitted, to the SPV. To be effective, that might also require assignment of the relevant trade names and trademarks. In addition, one must address performance of the obligations of the SPV as franchisor.[8] These issues are beyond the scope of this monograph.

The rejection of an executory contract by an originator in bankruptcy would subject the originator to a claim for damages for breach of contract. That damage claim, however, has no priority and ranks at parity with the originator's general unsecured claims. Presumably the claim would be worth less (perhaps far less) than 100 cents on the dollar.[9]

The foregoing analysis of risks was illustrated by reference to a payment stream represented by a franchise contract. The same legal conclusions would obtain, however, for other types of future payment streams — such as leases and licenses — where a contract

---

8. As demonstrated by the Days Inn franchise fee securitization transaction (see the discussion at pages 10–13), payment streams that are dependent upon the ongoing unique skills of, or services provided by, the originator may be more difficult to securitize.

9. *See* 11 U.S.C.A. § 365(g) (West 1979 & Supp. 1992) (hereinafter, title 11 sections are cited as the Bankruptcy Code). There is a further question that could arise in bankruptcy. Bankruptcy Code section 552(a) provides, in part, that property acquired by a company after the commencement of a bankruptcy case is not subject to a lien resulting from a prebankruptcy security agreement. Section 552(b) provides that proceeds of prebankruptcy property may be exempt from that restriction. Where the SPV pays for a future payment stream, such as lease rentals, would the SPV be entitled to rentals paid after the originator goes bankrupt? At least one court has said yes, holding that the net amount of payments received after bankruptcy under a prebankruptcy coal supply contract were proceeds subject to a prebankruptcy lien, even where the bankrupt company would have to continue to supply the coal in order to be paid. United Va. Bank v. Slab Fork Coal Co. (*In re* Slab Fork Coal Co.), 784 F.2d 1188, 1190–91 (4th Cir.), *cert. denied*, 477 U.S. 905 (1986) (following *In re* Sunberg, 729 F.2d 561 [8th Cir. 1984]). Because section 552(b) on its face allows a court to weigh the equities of each case, there is no assurance that a similar result will obtain in each case. In practice, however, courts generally have permitted claims of secured creditors against postpetition proceeds of prepetition collateral except to the extent of costs and expenses incurred by the debtor postpetition in generating such proceeds. *See, e.g., In re* Colonial Realty Inv. Co., 516 F.2d 154 (1st Cir. 1975).

Structured Finance

breach by the originator could raise a defense to payment by the obligors or where the contract is an executory contract.[10]

The recent voluntary bankruptcy filing by a major motel franchisor and its affiliates (which included an SPV formed to securitize its future franchise fees) illustrates both the structural strengths and possible weaknesses of securitizations of future payment streams. In September 1991, Days Inn of America, Inc. (DIA) and certain of its affiliates each filed a voluntary petition under chapter 11 of the Bankruptcy Code.[11] Days Inn Receivables Funding Corp. (DIRF), one of those affiliates, was a "bankruptcy-remote" SPV[12] created in 1988 to acquire from DIA (through a subsidiary of DIA) franchise agreements and franchise fees payable thereunder, as well as the Days Inn trademarks and trade names, the computer reservation systems, and certain other related property (the "Days Inn System"). DIRF then issued notes secured by a security interest in the Days Inn System.

After the chapter 11 filings, these debtors sought to sell the Days Inn System to a third party pursuant to section 363(b) of the Bankruptcy Code.[13] In their request for bankruptcy court approval of the

---

10. The nature of the receivable also can affect predictability of payment when the receivables are prepayable. If, for example, the receivables consisted of mortgage loans, and interest rates declined, the obligors might prepay the loans. Although the collections then should be sufficient to prepay the principal amount of the debt securities issued by the SPV, the holders of those securities may have bargained to have their securities outstanding for a longer period of time at a fixed interest rate. The problems associated with prepayments are beyond the scope of this monograph.
11. *In re* Days Inn of Am., Inc., Consol. Case Nos. 91-978 through 91- 986 inclusive (Bankr. D. Del. Sept. 27, 1991) (hereinafter DIA Bankruptcy Filing).
12. DIA caused DIRF to file for voluntary bankruptcy despite DIA's admission in the filing that DIRF was solvent at the time and was intended to be "bankruptcy-remote." *See infra* note 26 for a more detailed analysis of bankruptcy-remote SPVs.
13. Section 363(b)(1) the Bankruptcy Code provides that "[t]he trustee, after notice and a hearing, may use, sell or lease, other than in the ordinary course of business, property of the estate." Absent a formal plan of reorganization under chapter 11, courts have allowed a sale of substantially all of a debtor's assets under section 363 when there is a "sound business justification" therefor. *See, e.g., In re* Lionel Corp., 722 F.2d 1063, 1070–71 (2d Cir. 1983); *In re* Ionosphere Clubs, Inc., 100 B.R. 670, 675 (Bankr. S.D.N.Y. 1989).

Asset Securitization

sale, the debtors stated how the sale proceeds would be allocated among the various creditors. Because the DIRF secured noteholders would not be paid in full under the proposed allocation and, as a result of the proposed sale of the Days Inn System, their security interest therein would be adversely affected, the secured noteholders had a right under section 363(e) of the Bankruptcy Code to request the bankruptcy court to restrict the sale as necessary to provide "adequate protection of such interest."[14] Rather than so objecting, however, the secured noteholders agreed to settle their claims against DIRF for payment of slightly less than full value despite such claims' being oversecured. The secured noteholders apparently were willing to settle at a discount because they were concerned that the bankruptcy (as well as the inevitable delay and cost that any litigation would entail, even if successful) could have a detrimental effect on the value of the Days Inn System.[15]

Pursuant to the settlement agreement, however, the debtors effectively acknowledged the validity of the structure of the securitization.[16] The assignment of the Days Inn System to DIRF was never

---

14. Section 363(e) of the Bankruptcy Code provides that "[n]otwithstanding any other provision of [section 363], on request of an entity that has an interest in property ... sold ... or proposed to be ... sold ... by the trustee, the court, with or without a hearing, shall prohibit or condition such ... sale ... as is necessary to provide adequate protection of such interest."
15. Response of LaSalle National Bank as Successor Indenture Trustee to the Motion of Certain Debtors pursuant to Bankruptcy Code Section 363, DIA Bankr. Filing (Dec. 16, 1992) (hereinafter Noteholder Response). Pursuant to the settlement, the secured noteholders received an amount equal to the sum of (1) 95 percent of the outstanding principal of their secured notes, (2) accrued interest at the contractual predefault interest rate from the date of the last interest payment until closing of the settlement (including pre- and postpetition interest), and (3), in accordance with section 506(b) of the Bankruptcy Code, the reasonable expenses of the indenture trustee, the various committees representing the secured noteholders, their financial advisers, and their counsel.
16. *Id.* at 6 n.3. The settlement agreement provided that the debtors and the Original Committee of Unsecured Creditors acknowledged (1) the validity, priority, and effect for all purposes of the secured noteholders' security interest in the Days Inn System; (2) that the secured noteholders were oversecured; and (3) that all payments previously made on or in respect of the secured notes and a related loan and

challenged, and there was no attempt to "substantively consolidate" the assets of DIRF with those of the other debtors. (See the discussion under "Protecting the SPV from Substantive Consolidation.")

In short, the Days Inn bankruptcy illustrated both strengths and weaknesses in the structure. There were, in essence, two weaknesses. First, DIRF's single independent director voted to put the SPV into bankruptcy. As discussed below under "Protecting the SPV from Voluntary and Involuntary Bankruptcy," in light of new case law defining a director's fiduciary obligations to creditors in the vicinity of insolvency, an independent director of an SPV today should be less likely to vote for bankruptcy. Second, because of the length of time needed to repay the secured noteholders from collection of future franchise fees, the originator's bankruptcy raised a practical concern[17] regarding valuation of the receivables sufficient to induce the secured noteholders to settle at a small discount for an immediate payment. The possibility of linkage of the value of the receivables (including the ability to service and collect the receivables) to the

---

security agreement "were properly made in the ordinary course of business and cannot be avoided under applicable law," and shall not be challenged by the other parties to the settlement "as being preferential, or for any other reason."

17. Despite the fact that the Days Inn System was assigned to DIRF, the unique skills of the DIA personnel were perceived by existing and potential franchisees as being critical to the value of their Days Inn franchises. Additionally, the publicity from the bankruptcy was perceived by franchisees as being detrimental to business, and the time required by DIA personnel to attend to matters related to the bankruptcy distracted them from providing the services required under the franchise agreements. Existing and potential franchisees were reluctant to renew or enter into franchise contracts, and some existing franchisees claimed that the bankruptcy was a defense to their payment of franchise fees. *See, e.g.,* Noteholder Response 7 ("there may exist some danger that absent a speedy sale of the [Days Inn System] to a financially sound purchaser relations with franchisees might deteriorate, and the [Days Inn System] might lose the ability to retain present franchisees and attract new franchisees. In such circumstances, the value of the [Days Inn System] might substantially diminish, and it might be difficult to attract a purchaser for the Days Inn System, or to effect a successful reorganization"). Despite legally separating DIA from the Days Inn System, as a practical matter these factors linked the collateral value of the Days Inn System to DIA, including DIA's ability to perform under the franchise contracts.

Asset Securitization

health of the originator is an issue that should be carefully analyzed in every structured finance transaction.

On the other hand, Days Inn also illustrated some of the strengths of structured financing. The secured noteholders were repaid promptly with only a slight discount. Also, as mentioned, no attempts were made to substantively consolidate DIRF, or to invalidate the assignment of the Days Inn System as a fraudulent conveyance.[18] There is little doubt that had DIRF itself been able to avoid bankruptcy, or (even if DIRF were in bankruptcy) had the receivables been short-term assets, the secured noteholders may well have ended up with full payment of their claims.[19]

Financial Guarantees and Credit Supports

Sometimes the risk of predictability of payment is addressed by third-party credit enhancement.[20] That can take various forms, such as a guaranty or surety bond, a bank letter of credit, an irrevocable credit line, or the purchase by a third party of a tranche of subordinated securities from the SPV.[21] The goal is that a creditworthy party ensures payment of all or a portion of the securities issued by the

---

18. *See* discussion under "Separating the Source of Payment from the Originator."
19. *Cf.* Order Approving Settlement and Compromise, DIA Bankr. Filing 14-15 (Dec. 20, 1991): "[A]bsent the Settlement Agreement, any challenge to the extent of the DIRF noteholders' secured claims would likely entail burdensome, protracted and highly complex litigation with respect to the appropriate valuation of the DIRF noteholders' collateral. Such litigation would unquestionably have a negative impact on the proposed sale of the [Days Inn System], and result in a lower purchase price — all to the detriment of creditors and the Debtors' estates."
20. *See generally* Schwarcz & Varges, *Guaranties and Other Third Party Credit Supports, in* COMMERCIAL LOAN DOCUMENTATION GUIDE ch 4. (1989) (hereinafter Schwarcz & Varges).
21. The purchase by a third party of a tranche of subordinated securities (sometimes referred to as a "senior/subordinate" structure) actually is different from the other forms of third-party credit enhancement mentioned above. The creditworthiness of the buyer of the subordinated securities is unimportant. See discussion below. In cases where the originator, as opposed to a true third party, retains the subordinated securities, there often is not a true senior/subordinate structure but merely recourse to the originator by another name.

SPV. A rating agency that rates the SPV's securities would want the third party to be at least as creditworthy as the rating on the securities. The third party providing the credit support would want to be comfortable, as a business matter, with the ability to be repaid from the originator or its assets. If the third party has a claim for repayment that is enforceable against the originator or its general assets (as opposed, for example, to a subrogation claim limited to the receivables sold), the transaction may appear to provide a form of indirect recourse against the originator. Compare pages 31–32.

When the securities issued by the SPV are sold in a public offering, it is not uncommon to see a third party, typically rated AAA by Standard & Poor's Corp. and Aaa by Moody's Investors Service, Inc. (or the equivalent by other nationally recognized rating agencies, such as Fitch Investors Service, Inc. and Duff and Phelps), take at least a portion of the risk of nonpayment. For example, the third party may issue a surety bond or other financial guaranty in support of the securities issued by the SPV, causing such securities to be rated AAA/Aaa. That often would occur where the receivables are novel or do not have a well-established record of payment. The financial guaranty, although costly, provides the assurance needed to sell the SPV's securities in the public markets at investment-grade prices. Entities that are well known for providing those financial guarantees include Financial Security Assurance Inc. (FSA), Capital Markets Assurance Corp. (CapMAC), and Financial Guaranty Insurance Co. (FGIC).

Recently, as many institutions have experienced downgradings in the ratings on their long-term debt securities, new ways have been found to achieve credit enhancement that is not dependent on such ratings. For example, if an investor purchases a tranche of subordinated securities from the SPV, the creditworthiness of the investor (assuming the investor is independent of the other parties to the transaction) should be irrelevant. The cash the SPV receives by selling the subordinated securities enables the SPV to buy additional receivables from the originator. Because collections on the SPV's receivables, including these additional receivables, would be applied

Asset Securitization

(in accordance with the terms of the subordination) to pay the SPV's senior securities before the subordinated securities are paid, the issuance of the subordinated securities will have the effect of overcollateralizing the senior securities. An investor may be willing to purchase the subordinated securities, even though subordinated securities are riskier than senior securities, because the return, or yield, on the subordinated securities typically would be higher than the yield on the senior securities.

Another way to achieve credit enhancement that is not directly tied to a third party's credit rating is the so-called cash collateral account. A bank, for example, may be prepared to issue a letter of credit to back an SPV's securities. However, the bank's long-term credit rating may be insufficient to justify the desired rating on the securities. Instead of issuing a letter of credit, the bank[22] could fund a subordinated loan to the SPV. The SPV then would pledge the loan proceeds as collateral for its securities.

Because a cash collateral account is fully funded, it would be costlier than a letter of credit. On the other hand, investors may prefer the comfort provided by a cash collateral account as opposed to a letter of credit issued by a bank, which may be downgraded during the life of the transaction. Further, funding a cash collateral account is a method by which many banks can support a higher rating on an SPV's securities than would be obtainable through letters of credit issued by such banks. If the savings to the SPV in issuing higher-rated securities offsets the extra cost of a cash collateral account, a cash collateral account may well be an attractive alternative.

---

22. A cash collateral account is particularly useful when funded by a bank or other entity (such as, perhaps, an insurance company) that is not subject to federal bankruptcy law. *See* Bankruptcy Code § 109. If the cash collateral account were funded by an entity that later went bankrupt, arguments could be made that the loan might be voidable as a fraudulent conveyance or that the pledged loan proceeds constituted property of the bankrupt entity.

Structured Finance

Separating the Source of Payment from the Originator

We have previously discussed the "source" of payment. The source of payment must be *separated* from the originator in the event the originator becomes troubled or bankrupt. It is therefore necessary, first, to ensure that whatever happens to the originator cannot affect the SPV (often referred to as making the SPV "bankruptcy-remote"), and, second, to ensure that the transfer of the receivables from the originator to the SPV cannot be interfered with (often referred to as creating a "true sale" of the receivables).

Making the SPV "Bankruptcy-Remote"

The SPV itself must be insulated, to the extent practicable, from a possible bankruptcy of the originator. There are several ways the originator's bankruptcy could affect the SPV, and each must be protected against.

Protecting the SPV from Voluntary and Involuntary Bankruptcy

If the SPV is owned or controlled by the originator,[23] the originator may have the power to cause the SPV to file a voluntary petition for bankruptcy under section 301 of the Bankruptcy Code.[24] There are no legal standards that ordinarily must be met for a voluntary petition to be filed, nor does the Bankruptcy Code require any special procedures for a company to file a voluntary bankruptcy petition. A company would make this decision the way it would make any other significant decision. Unless restricted in its charter or bylaws, a corporation, for example, normally would make this decision by a vote of its board of directors.[25] It is therefore important to limit, by de-

---

23. Sometimes, for example, the SPV is a limited-purpose subsidiary of the originator. See discussion below of the FINCO, or two-tiered, structure.
24. Bankruptcy Code § 301.
25. *See* Price v. Gurney, 324 U.S. 100, 107 (1947).

16

Asset Securitization

sign, the ability of the originator to cause the SPV to file a petition for voluntary bankruptcy.[26]

This limitation normally is accomplished by drafting the SPV's charter or articles of incorporation or other organizational documents to restrict the circumstances under which it may file a voluntary petition for bankruptcy. Charters of SPVs usually provide that the SPV may not place itself into bankruptcy unless a requisite number of *independent* members of the board of directors vote for bankruptcy. An independent director, for example, might be defined as a person who is not a director (other than being a director of the SPV), officer, employee, or holder of 5 percent or more of the voting securities of the originator or any of the originator's affiliates. Such an independent director theoretically would be less influenced by the originator and more likely to consider his or her fiduciary obligations when required to vote for or against the SPV's bankruptcy. The independent-director requirement should help to insulate the SPV from the originator's bankruptcy, particularly in circumstances in which a director's fiduciary duties run to the SPV's creditors under the law of the particular jurisdiction of the SPV's formation.[27]

---

26. It appears to be against public policy to remove entirely a company's power to place itself in voluntary bankruptcy. *See* Fallick v. Kehr, 369 F.2d 899, 904–05 (2d Cir. 1966) (federal bankruptcy law reflects a strong legislative intent that debtors be allowed to get a fresh start); *In re* Tru Block Concrete Prods., Inc., 27 B.R. 486, 492 (Bankr. S.D. Cal. 1983) (prepetition agreement to avoid bankruptcy proceedings is void as against public policy); *In re* Adana Mortgage Bankers, Inc., 12 B.R. 989, 1009 (N.D. Ga. 1980) (even a bargained-for and knowledgeable waiver of right to seek protection of bankruptcy law is void); *In re* Weitzen, 3 F. Supp. 698, 698–99 (S.D.N.Y. 1933) (agreement to waive benefits of bankruptcy is unenforceable).

27. Although some states have statutes permitting a corporation's board of directors to consider the rights of third parties ("constituency statutes"), in the majority of jurisdictions the courts have found that the officers and directors of a corporation have a duty to the corporation and its shareholders. *See, e.g.,* Revlon, Inc. v. MacAndrews & Forbes Holdings, 506 A.2d 173, 179 (Del. 1986). Creditors are protected by their bargained-for contract rights, and usually are not owed a fiduciary duty. *See* Pepper v. Litton, 308 U.S. 295 (1939). However, once such a corporation becomes, or is on the brink of becoming, insolvent, in the majority of jurisdictions the courts recognize that fiduciary duties are owed to the corporation's creditors as well. *See, e.g.,* Katz v. Oak Indus., 508 A.2d 873 (Del. Ch. 1986). Further, a recent case, Credit Ly-

Some SPVs are organized with at least two classes of stock; and both classes must vote affirmatively for bankruptcy in order for the SPV to file a voluntary petition. One class of stock then is pledged to, or otherwise controlled by, the holders of the SPV's securities.[28] If, however, the holders of the SPV's securities control, by pledge or otherwise, a class of the SPV's voting stock, there may be a question

---

onnais Bank v. Pathé Communications, No. 12150, 199 WL 277613 (Del. Ch. Dec. 30, 1991), held that the directors of a Delaware corporation operating in the "vicinity" of insolvency were not merely agents of the shareholders, but instead owed a fiduciary duty to the corporate enterprise, including creditors. For a detailed discussion of this case and its application to structured finance, *see* Schwarcz, *Credit Lyonnais Case Clarifies ABS [Asset-Based Securities] Issues in Bankruptcy,* ASSET SALES REP., Oct. 12, 1992, at 1. The author essentially concludes that an SPV, whether or not technically insolvent, that is owned by an originator that is in or about to file bankruptcy would appear to be in the "vicinity of insolvency" within the meaning of this case. The directors therefore would be required, under their resulting fiduciary duty to creditors as well as shareholders, to consider voting against a voluntary bankruptcy of the SPV in most situations.

28. *See, e.g., In re* Sea-Land Corp. Shareholders Litig., Fed. Sec. L. Rep. (CCH) ¶ 93,923 (Del. Ch. 1988); Aronson v. Lewis, 473 A.2d 805, 815–17 (Del. 1984); Gilbert v. El Paso Co., 490 A.2d 1050 (Ch. 1984), *aff'd,* 575 A.2d 1131 (Del. 1990), for a discussion by the Delaware courts of what constitutes shareholder control and the type of liability that might accompany such control. Related to this is the issue of whether the holders of the SPV's securities may vote against a bankruptcy proceeding for the SPV when such a proceeding might be in the best interests of the equity owner of the SPV (i.e., the originator). Courts have held that when a creditor is able to exercise control of a corporation by voting pledged securities, it has a duty to use reasonable care to maintain the value of the collateral. *See, e.g.,* Citibank, N.A. v. Data Lease Fin. Corp., 838 F.2d 686, 694 (11th Cir. 1987), *cert. denied,* 108 S. Ct. 1019 (1988); Empire Life Ins. Co. of Am. v. Valdak Corp., 468 F.2d 330, 335 (5th Cir. 1972). But the creditor nonetheless has the right to protect its legitimate self-interest and need not fall back upon its debtor's recommendations in order to satisfy the duty of reasonable care. Bankers Trust Co. v. J.V. Dowler & Co., 390 N.E.2d 766 (N.Y. 1979). In addition, because there are no clear authorities distinguishing the approach of using two classes of stock from a prepetition agreement to waive the benefits of bankruptcy (*cf.* note 26 *supra*), the charters of some SPVs require the vote of both classes only if the SPV is solvent; if the SPV is insolvent, the affirmative vote of the class of stock pledged to security holders would not be required. For a discussion of these issues in the context of legal opinions, *see* Special Report by the TriBar Opinion Committee, *Opinions in the Bankruptcy Context: Rating Agency, Structured Financing and Chapter 11 Transactions,* 46 BUS. LAW. 718 (1991) (hereinafter Special Report by the TriBar Opinion Committee).

Asset Securitization

whether those holders are exposed to liability claims for "controlling" the SPV, although the risk arguably can be minimized by limiting that class's voting rights solely to the question of whether or not to file the voluntary bankruptcy petition.

These methods are not infallible. For example, as discussed on pages 10–13, in September 1991 Days Inn Receivables Funding Corp. (DIRF), a "bankruptcy-remote" SPV that was solvent at the time, filed for voluntary bankruptcy together with certain of its affiliates.[29] The bankruptcy filing was intended to facilitate the sale of the assets securing DIRF's secured notes pursuant to section 363(b) of the Bankruptcy Code.[30]

DIRF's charter required an independent director on its board, and also required the unanimous vote of DIRF's directors (including the independent director) in order to file for voluntary bankruptcy. In addition, so long as any of DIRF's secured notes remained unpaid, DIRF's charter required the consent of the indenture trustee for the notes in order to file a voluntary bankruptcy. Nonetheless, DIRF's independent director voted for the voluntary bankruptcy filing despite DIRF's being solvent, and the indenture trustee's consent was not obtained for the filing.[31]

Regardless of whether DIRF's directors acted properly in voting to file for the voluntary bankruptcy,[32] DIRF's charter could have been

---

29. Bergner Credit Corp., a "bankruptcy-remote" SPV formed to securitize credit card receivables of several of its affiliates, also filed for voluntary bankruptcy in conjunction with its parent and several of its affiliates. *In re* P.A. Bergner & Co. Holding Co., Consol. Case Nos. 91-05501 through 91-05516 inclusive (1991).
30. Memorandum of Law in Support of Joint Motion for Order Authorizing Debtors to Sell Certain Assets Pursuant to Section 363 of the Bankruptcy Code and Assume Certain Executory Contracts in Connection with the Proposed Sale, Consol. Case Nos. 91-978 through 91-986 inclusive (Dec. 19, 1991).
31. If the indenture trustee had objected to the voluntary bankruptcy on the grounds that its consent was not so obtained, it is likely that a court, as a matter of public policy, would have voided the consent requirement as an excessive restriction on DIRF's right to the benefits of bankruptcy protection. *See* discussion at note 26 *supra*.
32. *See* the discussion at note 27 *supra*. In the article on the recent *Credit Lyonnais* case referred to in note 27, the author concluded that had "the *Credit Lyonnais* case . . . been decided at the time of the Days Inn bankruptcy, the directors of [DIRF] would

Structured Finance

designed to provide greater insulation from the bankruptcies of its affiliates. For example, the charters of many recently formed SPVs require at least two independent directors on the board while retaining the requirement that each director's affirmative vote is necessary in order to file for voluntary bankruptcy. Some charters also restrict an SPV from filing a voluntary bankruptcy if it is solvent at the time.[33]

In addition to the foregoing methods for insulating an SPV from the originator's bankruptcy, under certain limited circumstances it may be appropriate to require the control person of the originator to execute a "springing" guaranty of the SPV's securities as a condition of such securities' issuance. Pursuant to its terms, that guaranty would become effective only if the SPV filed a voluntary petition for bankruptcy while it was solvent and able to pay its debts.[34] Thus, the springing guaranty would provide the control person of the originator with a disincentive to causing the SPV to file a voluntary bankruptcy.[35] The extra degree of protection provided by the springing guaranty approach could be especially useful for structured financings involving long-term assets, such as patents, trademarks, and trade names, that have value to the originator significantly in excess of the amount of the financing.[36] However, a springing guaranty must be carefully structured to avoid triggering other bankruptcy risks.[37]

---

have been more clearly obligated to consider their fiduciary duty to the security noteholders," and that "applying the logic of the *Credit Lyonnais* case, the directors of [DIRF] arguably . . . should be obligated to vote against bankruptcy unless (for example, through a prepackaged bankruptcy) there are appropriate assurances that the securitized noteholders will obtain full and timely payment."

33. Although it is uncertain as a matter of law whether such a restriction is enforceable, restricting a solvent (as opposed to insolvent) SPV's right to file a voluntary bankruptcy would appear to be less objectionable on public policy grounds. *See* discussion at notes 26 and 31.
34. The term "springing" guaranty refers to its springing into effectiveness upon such an event.
35. *See Days Inns' SPC Filing Spawns Securitization Poison Pill,* ASSET SALES REP., Nov. 25, 1991, at 1.
36. As the Days Inn bankruptcy demonstrated, putting the SPV into bankruptcy could help to facilitate the sale of a long-term asset, thereby allowing the originator to realize the value of the asset immediately.
37. *See* article cited in note 35 above.

Asset Securitization

Another approach is for the SPV to be neither owned nor controlled by the originator. The SPV may, for example, be owned by an independent third party, such as a charitable institution. If the SPV continued to collect the receivables and pay on its securities even after the originator went bankrupt, the charity (or other third party) would have no incentive to place the SPV in bankruptcy. An independent SPV, however, may not be as useful as a subsidiary SPV, except as part of a "FINCO," or "two-tiered," structure.[38] That is because, in order to achieve a bankruptcy-remote structure, the transfer of receivables from the originator to the independent SPV would have to be a "true sale." But to achieve a true sale, the level of recourse created through overcollateralization cannot be excessive; and whatever level of overcollateralization is required to give investors comfort may well also give rise to a tension with the originator, which ideally would like a return of collections on the sold receivables once the securities issued by the SPV are paid in full. Further, because a "true sale" of receivables for bankruptcy almost certainly will constitute a sale of such receivables for tax purposes, the originator would be required to recognize gain or loss on the sale (see pages 46–49). The FINCO, or two-tiered, structure offers solutions to these problems.

In the FINCO structure, the originator transfers receivables to a wholly owned bankruptcy-remote subsidiary (SPV$_1$), in part pursuant to a true sale and (to achieve the necessary level of overcollateralization) in part through a capital contribution. The contribution to capital should survive any fraudulent conveyance attack by the originator's trustee-in-bankruptcy because the subsidiary is wholly owned.[39] But because SPV$_1$ would be part of the originator's consolidated tax group for federal (but not necessarily state — the rules vary) tax purposes, so far there is no taxable transfer, at least under federal law.[40]

---

38. *See* discussion on pages 22–23.
39. *See* discussion under "Protecting Against the Fraudulent Conveyance Risk." *Cf.* Special Report by the TriBar Opinion Committee, *supra* note 28, at 727–29.
40. *See* the discussion on page 48.

21

Structured Finance

If SPV$_1$ itself were to issue debt securities to investors, the debt would be required to be recorded on its balance sheet, which, pursuant to generally accepted accounting principles, must be consolidated with the originator's balance sheet.[41] The originator nonetheless could achieve "off-balance-sheet" treatment either by issuing securities that are not required to be recorded as debt or, for example, by causing SPV$_1$ to transfer its receivables to a separate and independent bankruptcy-remote SPV (SPV$_2$)[42] in a manner structured to constitute a sale of the receivables for accounting purposes but a loan secured by the receivables for tax purposes.[43] SPV$_2$, which is independent, then could issue debt securities to investors to fund the transfer of such receivables without affecting the liability side of the originator's balance sheet.

The result is effectively to separate the transferred receivables from the originator's bankruptcy, thereby permitting the originator to obtain low-cost off-balance-sheet financing without the originator's having to recognize loss or gain for federal tax purposes. Further, any "upside" from collections of the receivables, once the investors in the securities issued by SPV$_2$ are paid in full, can be captured by the originator: because the transaction between SPV$_1$ and SPV$_2$ is (for purposes other than accounting) a loan, SPV$_1$ would be entitled to any such upside; and the originator later could merge SPV$_1$ into itself to capture that upside.

The SPV also could be structured as an entity that cannot become the subject of a bankruptcy case. One such entity is a trust,[44] al-

---

41. Financial Accounting Standards Board (FASB), Statement of Financial Accounting Standards No. 94.
42. SPV$_2$ also could agree to purchase the receivables on an ongoing basis.
43. *See* the discussion on page 47.
44. Originators seeking flexibility in financing options recently have been considering a "master trust." As with traditional asset securitizations, the originator would transfer (directly or through a FINCO structure) receivables to the master trust, and the master trust would issue certificates representing undivided interests in those receivables. The master trust, however, can be structured to be able to issue different classes and series of certificates over time. In addition, the master trust can be permitted, under certain conditions, to add or remove receivables from the trust.

Asset Securitization

though "business trusts" may be the subject of bankruptcy cases.[45] If the originator is an entity, such as a bank, that cannot become the subject of a bankruptcy case, the requirements for an SPV may be more lenient, since bankruptcy is not a risk.[46]

Thus, a master trust can permit an originator to obtain different types of ongoing financing for its receivables without having to establish a new structure each time.

45. Section 109 of the Bankruptcy Code provides that only a *person* may be eligible for relief under the Bankruptcy Code. Section 101(41) of the Bankruptcy Code defines a "person" to include a "corporation," and section 101(9)(A)(v) of the Bankruptcy Code defines a corporation to include a "business trust." Although the Bankruptcy Code does not define the term "business trust," the courts have adopted several different interpretations of the term, all of which could include an SPV, depending on its structure. *See, e.g., In re* Heritage N. Dunlap Trust, 120 B.R. 252, 254 (Bankr. D. Mass. 1990) (whether a trust is a "business trust" is determined by looking to applicable state law [including filing and registration requirements]); *In re* Michigan Real Estate Ins. Trust, 87 B.R. 447, 449 (E.D. Mich. 1988) ("[a] business trust is 'an unincorporated business organization . . . by which property is to be held and managed by trustees for the benefit and profit of such persons as may be or may become the holders of transferable certificates evidencing the beneficial interests in the trust's estate'") (citing 13 AM. JUR. 2D *Business Trusts* § 1); *In re* Mosby, 61 B.R. 636, 638 (E.D. Mo. 1985), *aff'd,* 791 F.2d 628 (8th Cir. 1986) (relied on cases with respect to business trusts in the federal tax context); *In re* Universal Clearing House Co., 60 B.R. 985, 992 (D. Utah 1986) (debtor found to be a business trust because its express purpose was making profit rather than protecting the trust assets). In addition, when defining a "corporation" the drafters of the Bankruptcy Code inserted the term "business trust" in place of the following language used in the Bankruptcy Act of 1898: "any business conducted by a trustee or trustees wherein beneficial interest or ownership is evidenced by a certificate or other written instrument." Because at least one court has noted that this change was intended by Congress to broaden the variety of trusts eligible to obtain relief in the bankruptcy courts, it is quite possible that an SPV in the form of trust issuing securities or certificates would be considered a "business trust." *See In re* Tru Block Concrete Prods., Inc., 27 B.R. 486, 490–91 (S.D. Cal. 1983). *See also* Hecht v. Malley, 265 U.S. 144, 159–62 (1924); W. FLETCHER, 16A FLETCHER'S CYCLOPEDIA OF THE LAW OF PRIVATE CORPORATIONS § 8267 (D. Nelson & M. Wasiunec rev. ed., 1988). *See* Bankruptcy Code § 101(8)(A)(v). Therefore, even if a trust is used, it may be prudent to include it as part of a FINCO structure with the trust being used in place of SPV$_2$, to ensure that the trust's assets do not become part of the originator's estate in bankruptcy.

46. *See* Bankruptcy Code § 109. Banks are subject, however, to applicable federal or state laws and regulations regarding their financial condition that would apply in lieu of federal bankruptcy law.

Structured Finance

Once the SPV's power to file a voluntary bankruptcy petition is restricted, the next step is to limit the circumstances under which creditors can force the SPV into involuntary bankruptcy. Unlike the case in voluntary bankruptcy, a creditor may not force an SPV into involuntary bankruptcy unless the SPV meets the criteria required for filing.[47] These criteria are that the SPV is either generally not paying its debts as they become due, or that a custodian (other than a trustee, receiver, or agent appointed or authorized to take charge of less than substantially all of the property of the SPV for the purpose of enforcing a lien against such property) has been appointed or has taken possession.[48] One therefore may attempt to protect against involuntary bankruptcy by limiting both the debt that the SPV can issue and the number of its trade creditors. (The number of trade creditors can be effectively limited by limiting the business in which the SPV can engage.) These limitations could be included, for example, in the SPV's charter or other organizational documents. Further, any third parties that deal with the SPV contractually could be required to waive their rights to file an involuntary bankruptcy petition against the SPV.

Protecting the SPV from Substantive Consolidation

Eliminating creditors does not guarantee that the SPV will be protected from the originator's bankruptcy. An equitable doctrine of law, known as substantive consolidation, may allow a court under appropriate circumstances to consolidate the assets and liabilities of the originator and the SPV.[49] Although substantive consolidation usually arises in the context of the bankruptcy of both the originator and the

---

47. Section 303(b) of the Bankruptcy Code also has requirements for the number of creditors and the types of claims necessary for filing an involuntary petition.
48. *See* Bankruptcy Code § 303(h).
49. A court also could jointly administer the bankruptcy cases of affiliated debtors. *See* FED. R. BANKR. P. 1015(b). That would *not* affect the substantive rights of debtors or creditors, but would be intended solely for administrative convenience where multiple affiliated debtors are in bankruptcy.

Asset Securitization

SPV, a court could order a substantive consolidation even if the SPV were not in bankruptcy.[50]

Courts do not order substantive consolidation lightly. The determination that two entities should be substantively consolidated must be made on a case-by-case basis, after consideration of the relevant facts of each case. Courts will take into consideration both the nature of the relationship between the entities to be consolidated and the effect of the consolidation on the creditors of each entity. The courts have identified the following among the factors to be considered for this purpose:

1. The degree of difficulty in segregating and ascertaining individual liabilities and assets;
2. The presence or absence of consolidated financial statements;
3. The commingling of assets and business functions;
4. The unity of ownership and interests between the corporate entities;
5. The guaranteeing by the parent of loans of the subsidiary; and
6. The transfer of assets without formal observance of corporate formalities.[51]

The presence of some or even many of these factors does not, however, necessarily mean that a court will order a substantive consolidation. Courts have held that because substantive consolidation is an equitable remedy, it should not be used to harm innocent holders of securities of the company (in our case, the SPV) that is the target of consolidation.[52]

---

50. See, e.g., Sampsell v. Imperial Paper & Color Corp., 313 U.S. 215 (1941) (consolidating the assets of corporation with those of its shareholders); 5 WILLIAM MILLER COLLIER, COLLIER ON BANKRUPTCY ¶ 1100.06[3], at 1100-44 to -46 (15th ed. 1989).
51. See, e.g., In re Vecco Constr. Indus., 4 B.R. 407, 410 (Bankr. E.D. Va. 1980); see discussion in 5 WILLIAM MILLER COLLIER, COLLIER ON BANKRUPTCY ¶ 1100.06[3] (15th ed. 1989); Chemical Bank N.Y. Trust Co. v. Kheel (In re Seatrade Corp.), 369 F.2d 845, 847 (2d Cir. 1966); In re Manzey Land & Cattle Co., 17 B.R. 332, 338 (Bankr. D. S.D. 1982).
52. See, e.g., In re Augie/Restivo Baking Co., 860 F.2d 515 (2d Cir. 1988) (denying consolidation where one creditor would suffer unfairly); In re Snider Bros., 18

Structured Finance

It therefore would not appear likely that a court would substantively consolidate the assets and liabilities of an SPV and a bankrupt originator in a typical transaction. Nonetheless, substantive consolidation is an equitable remedy and is highly dependent on the facts.

Protecting the SPV from Governmental Claims

The foregoing discussion has focused on limiting the circumstances under which the SPV, or its assets, could become subject to bankruptcy. Certain types of governmental claims that arise against the originator, however, may also be asserted against the SPV, regardless of whether the SPV is in bankruptcy. Under the Internal Revenue Code, for example, a claim can be asserted against any member of a consolidated tax group.[53] If the SPV is a member of the originator's consolidated tax group, as would be likely if the SPV is a subsidiary of the originator, the Internal Revenue Service would be able to assert a claim that it has against the originator directly against the SPV.[54]

Another type of governmental claim that may be asserted in this way is a pension claim. Certain governmental claims relating to defined-benefit pension plans can be asserted under the Internal Revenue Code and the Employee Retirement Income Security Act of 1974, as amended (ERISA)[55] against any trade or business under common control with the sponsor of the plan (a "controlled

---

B.R. 230, 239 (Bankr. D. Mass. 1982) (court's power arises out of equity and should be used sparingly).

53. I.R.C. § 1502 (West 1993).
54. Section 1.1502-6 of the Treasury Regulations states that the common parent corporation and each subsidiary that was a member of the group during any part of the consolidated return year will be severally liable for the tax for that year unless the subsidiary has ceased to be a part of the group as the result of a bona fide sale or exchange for fair value prior to the date upon which the deficiency was assessed, in which case such liability may be limited. No agreement entered into by one or more members of the group with any other member or other person can eliminate or reduce that liability. 26 C.F.R. § 1.1502-6 (1992).
55. Employee Retirement Income Security Act of 1974, Pub. L. No. 93-406, 88 Stat. 829 (codified as amended in scattered sections of 26 U.S.C. and 29 U.S.C.) (hereinafter ERISA).

Asset Securitization

group").[56] For example, if there are unfunded benefits payable upon the termination of a defined-benefit pension plan, the sponsoring employer and each member of its controlled group, which could include the SPV, would be liable to the Pension Benefit Guaranty Corporation (PBGC), the agency responsible for administering the ERISA plan-termination rules, for 100 percent of the unfunded benefits.[57] In addition, the PBGC has a lien for its claim against the property of each member of the group, up to 30 percent of the collective net worth of the group.[58] The lien generally has the same status as a tax lien.[59] In addition, liability for unpaid contributions to an ongoing defined-benefit pension plan extends to all members of the controlled group, and a lien on their property (with the same status as a tax lien) will be imposed in favor of the PBGC if the unpaid contributions exceed a certain level.[60] These governmental claims could have priority over claims of general unsecured creditors.

It is possible, however, for the claims of holders of securities of the SPV to gain priority over governmental claims by the SPV's pledging its receivables to secure repayment of the security holders. Such a pledge would come ahead of the governmental claims in most instances.[61]

---

56. In general, a controlled group includes parent-subsidiary and brother-sister groups that are under 80 percent common ownership, and therefore may include an 80 percent-owned SPV. I.R.C. § 414(b), (c) (West 1993); Treas. Reg. § 1.414(b), (c), 26 C.F.R. §§ 1, 602 (1992); ERISA § 4001(b), 88 Stat. at 1004 (codified as amended at 26 U.S.C. § 401).
57. ERISA § 4062(a), (b), 88 Stat. at 1029 (codified as amended at 29 U.S.C. § 1362[a], [b]).
58. ERISA § 4068(a), 88 Stat. at 1032 (codified as amended at 29 U.S.C. § 1368[a]). The PBGC generally has great latitude in determining net worth, and ERISA specifically provides that negative net worths of group members are *not* offset against positive net worths for these purposes. ERISA § 4062(d)(1)(A)(i), 88 Stat. at 1029 (codified as amended at 29 U.S.C. § 1362[d][1]).
59. ERISA § 4068(c), 88 Stat. at 1032–33 (codified as amended at 26 U.S.C. § 6323).
60. I.R.C. § 412(c)(11), (n) (West 1993); ERISA § 302(c), 88 Stat. at 871 (codified as amended at 29 U.S.C. § 1082[1][3]).
61. *See, e.g., In re* National Fin. Alternatives, Inc., 96 B.R. 844, 853–54 (Bankr. N.D. Ill. 1989) (holding that receivables acquired by the debtor after a tax lien filed by the IRS had become effective were nevertheless "qualified property," i.e., property

Structured Finance

Creating a "True Sale" of the Receivables

Having accomplished a separation of the originator and the SPV, it is important to ensure that ownership of the receivables is effectively transferred to the SPV. That transfer is typically referred to as a "true sale." The term "true sale" is misleading, however, because a given transfer of receivables may well be a sale for certain purposes but not others. For example, the criteria for establishing an accounting sale under generally accepted accounting principles (GAAP), governed by Statement of Financial Accounting Standards No. 77 (SFAS 77), are less stringent[62] than the criteria for establishing a sale under bankruptcy law.

The originator transferring its receivables to the SPV usually will want the transfer to constitute a sale for accounting purposes. That way the financing is reflected on its balance sheet as a sale of assets and not as a secured loan (which would increase leverage). The originator also may want the transfer to be a sale for purposes of its indenture covenants, if such covenants restrict the originator's ability to incur debt or pledge its assets. In many cases, particularly where

---

covered by the creditor's prior security interest, so long as they were the identifiable proceeds of a contract right acquired prior to the effective date of the tax lien and had not been commingled with other funds or expended to acquire other properties after that date. *Cf.* U.C.C. §§ 9-301(4), 9-312. Another issue, discussed at pages 49–51, is the extent to which the SPV may be subject to income tax.

62. On February 23, 1989, at a meeting of the FASB's Emerging Issues Task Force (EITF), the SEC observer stated that the SEC was becoming increasingly concerned about certain receivables, leasing, and other transactions involving special-purpose vehicles. The SEC observer suggested, for the EITF's consideration, certain requirements that the SEC felt should be met in order for the transfers of receivables to be recognized as sales and to avoid consolidation of the SPV and the originator of the receivables. These requirements included that the majority owner of the SPV be an independent third party who has made a substantive capital investment in the SPV, has control of the SPV, and has substantive risks and rewards of ownership of receivables or other assets purchased by the SPV (including residuals). Although the SEC staff said it was considering the issuance of a Staff Accounting Bulletin setting forth guidelines on the accounting for transactions involving SPVs, and until that time would consider transactions on a case-by-case basis, to date no such bulletin has been issued. *See EITF Abstracts* No. 84-30.

Asset Securitization

the indenture itself states that its interpretation is to be governed by GAAP, it may well be the case that a transfer that is an accounting sale also will be viewed as a sale under the indenture.[63] Whether a given transfer of receivables violates one or more indenture or other contractual covenants, however, is a legal question that turns closely on the precise contractual language, and usually would be best interpreted by the originator's own counsel.

The term "true sale" most often is used in analyzing whether the transfer of receivables effectively has removed the receivables from the originator for bankruptcy purposes. If the originator goes bankrupt and the receivables are no longer owned by the originator, but instead are owned by the SPV, then the SPV also would own the collections on the receivables. Assuming the receivables were paid, the SPV then would have sufficient cash to pay its securities without defaulting. If the transfer is held not to be a sale for bankruptcy purposes, it will be deemed an advance of funds by the SPV to the originator secured by the receivables.[64] The SPV would then be a creditor of the originator and have a security interest, but not an ownership interest, in the receivables. In such a case, the originator's bankruptcy would, under section 362 of the Bankruptcy Code, automatically result in a stay of all actions by creditors to foreclose on or otherwise obtain property of the originator.[65]

If the transfer of the receivables from the originator to the SPV is recharacterized by the bankruptcy court as a secured loan rather than

---

63. For example, the indenture covenant may restrict liens securing debt, although the term "debt" may not be defined in the indenture. Indentures often state that accounting terms used therein are to be construed in accordance with GAAP. A court therefore may use the GAAP definition of "debt," which is governed by SFAS 77.
64. *See* PETER H. WEIL, ASSET-BASED LENDING: A PRACTICAL GUIDE TO SECURED FINANCING 205–06 (2d ed. 1992) (hereinafter WEIL). A related issue is whether a true sale of receivables can be voided as a "fraudulent conveyance." See pages 35–36.
65. Section 362(d) provides criteria for the judge to determine whether to lift the stay. Whether the stay will be lifted depends on the facts of the given case. *See, e.g., In re* Comcoach Corp., 698 F.2d 571, 573–74 (2d Cir. 1983); *In re* Sweetwater, 11 Bankr. Ct. Dec. (CRR) 1220, 1227 (Bankr. 1984) *aff'd,* 57 B.R. 748 (D. Utah 1985).

as a sale, the SPV <u>may not be able to obtain payments collected on the receivables</u> until the stay is modified. Further, under section 363 of the Bankruptcy Code, a court, after notice to creditors and the opportunity of a hearing, could order the cash collections of the receivables to be used by the originator in its business as working capital if adequate protection of the interest of the SPV in the receivables is provided by the originator or its trustee.[66] "Adequate protection," though, does not necessarily translate into an alternative cash source.

In addition, section 364 of the Bankruptcy Code would permit the originator, if credit is not otherwise available to it and if adequate protection is given to the SPV, to raise cash by granting to new lenders a lien that is either *pari passu* with that of the SPV or, if a *pari passu* lien cannot attract new financing, having priority over the SPV's lien.[67]

---

66. "Adequate protection" is not defined in the Bankruptcy Code. Instead, section 361 of the Bankruptcy Code gives several examples of what may constitute adequate protection, such as making periodic cash payments to the creditor (§ 361[1]) or granting a lien on other unencumbered property in the debtor's estate (§ 361[2]), and leaves it for the courts to decide on a case-by-case basis what constitutes "adequate protection" in the circumstances. *See, e.g., In re* AIC Indus., 83 B.R. 774, 777 (Bankr. D. Colo. 1988) ("adequate protection" pursuant to section 363); *In re* O.P. Held, Inc., 74 B.R. 777, 782–84 (Bankr. N.D.N.Y. 1987). For a thorough discussion of the issue of "adequate protection," *see In re* Timbers of Inwood Forest Ass'n, 808 F.2d 363 (5th Cir. 1987), *aff'd*, 484 U.S. 365 (1989).

67. Section 364(d)(1) of the Bankruptcy Code provides as follows:

     The court, after notice and a hearing, may authorize the obtaining of credit or the incurring of debt secured by a senior or equal lien on property of the estate that is subject to a lien only if —
     (A) the trustee is unable to obtain such credit otherwise; and
     (B) there is adequate protection of the interest of the holder of the lien on the property of the estate on which such senior or equal lien is proposed to be granted.

    In practice, it is common for a secured lender in bankruptcy to work out an arrangement, approved by the court after notice and a hearing, whereby the lender in effect re-advances the cash collections it receives as new postpetition loans secured by future receivables for the company. For a discussion of these arrangements, *see* Harvey S. Schochet & Christine A. Murphy, *Financing the Debtor-in-Possession: Section 364 of the Bankruptcy Code, in* 1 ADVANCED BANKRUPTCY WORKSHOP: CASE STUDIES IN HANDLING CHAPTER 11 PROBLEMS 445 (PLI Commercial Law &

Asset Securitization

Although various courts have considered whether a given transfer of receivables constitutes a sale or a secured loan for bankruptcy purposes, the facts of the decided cases have not been representative for the most part of modern asset-securitized transactions. Accordingly, the cases are not easily harmonized, and different readers can argue as to which factors are relevant and which are entitled to the greater weight. Nonetheless, a cluster of factors can be identified that are relevant in most determinations of whether a given transfer of receivables is a sale or a secured loan. Each of these factors is indicative of whether the originator truly parted with the future economic risks and benefits of ownership of the receivables purported to be sold, and whether the SPV has taken on those risks and benefits.

Recourse

The most significant factor appears to be the extent of recourse the transferee of the receivables has against the transferor. As the degree of recourse increases, the likelihood that a court will find a true sale decreases. The existence of some recourse does not by itself preclude characterization of the transaction as a true sale. If recourse is present, the issue is "whether the *nature* of the recourse, and the true nature of the transaction, are such that the legal rights and economic consequences of the agreement bear a great similarity to a financing transaction [i.e., a secured loan] or to a sale."[68]

Sometimes the originator represents and warrants that all receivables sold meet certain eligibility criteria, and the originator will provide an indemnity for breach of those representations and warranties. To the extent the representations and warranties are not general representations and warranties of collectibility, but rather are limited to

---

Practice Course Handbook Series No. 448, 1988); Harvey S. Schochet et al., *Postpetition Financing: Section 364 of the Bankruptcy Code, in* 1 ADVANCED BANKRUPTCY WORKSHOP 1989, at 213 (PLI Commercial Law & Practice Course Handbook Series No. 487, 1989).

68. Major's Furniture Mart, Inc. v. Castle Credit Corp., 602 F.2d 538, 544 (3d Cir. 1979) (emphasis in original; footnotes omitted).

the condition of the receivables at the time the receivables are sold, that should not differ from a warranty ordinarily given by a seller of a product.[69] Accordingly, such limited representations and warranties and indemnity should not be inconsistent with sale treatment.

Retained Rights and Right to Surplus

Perhaps the second most important factor indicating a secured transaction is the originator's right to redeem or repurchase transferred receivables. For example, section 9-506 of the Uniform Commercial Code (UCC) and various state mortgage statutes allow a debtor to redeem property before it is ultimately disposed of by a secured party.[70] The absence of a right of redemption or repurchase would be a factor in favor of characterization of the receivables transaction as a true sale.

Several courts also have considered the existence of a transferor's right to any surplus collections, once the transferee has collected its investment plus an agreed yield, as indicative of a secured loan.[71] The right of the transferee of the receivables to retain all collections of transferred receivables for its own account, even after the transferee has collected its investment plus yield, would therefore be a factor in favor of characterization of the receivables transaction as a true sale.

Pricing Mechanism

Pricing based upon a fluctuating interest index of the type found in commercial loan agreements, such as the prime or base rate, may be indicative of a secured loan. The pricing mechanism also may be indicative of a secured loan to the extent the purchase price is retroac-

---

69. *See* U.C.C. §§ 2-312, 2-313, 2-314, 2-315.
70. *See, e.g.*, DEL. CODE ANN. tit. 6, § 9-506 (Supp. 1988).
71. *See, e.g., In re* Evergreen Valley Resort, Inc., 23 B.R. 659, 661–62 (Bankr. D. Me. 1982); *In re* Hurricane Elkhorn Coal Corp., 19 B.R. 609, 617 (Bankr. W.D. Ky. 1982), *rev'd on other grounds*, 763 F.2d 188 (6th Cir. 1985); *In re* Nixon Mach. Co., 6 B.R. 847, 854 (Bankr. E.D. Tenn. 1980).

Asset Securitization

tively adjusted to reflect actual rather than expected collections on receivables.[72]

In the closest approach to a true sale, the SPV would purchase receivables on a discounted basis. The discount would be calculated or negotiated prior to each purchase, in part based on the SPV's then net current cost of funds and the anticipated collection and loss experience of the receivables then to be purchased. Once a discount has been negotiated for each purchase, it would not thereafter be modified or otherwise adjusted for that purchase, regardless of differences between the actual and anticipated costs of funds and of collection experience. Such pricing would be a factor in favor of characterization of the receivables transaction as a true sale.

Administration and Collection of Accounts

The administration of and control over the collection of accounts receivable are factors sometimes cited by courts in resolving the sale/secured loan issue.[73] To have a true purchase, the transferee should have the authority to control the collection of the accounts.[74] Examples of such authority would include

(1) ownership by the transferee of all the books, records, and computer tapes relating to the purchased receivables and
(2) the transferee's having the right
   (a) to control the activities of any collection agent with respect to purchased receivables and at any time to appoint itself or another person as collection agent,
   (b) to establish a credit and collection policy with respect to purchased receivables, and
   (c) at any time to notify the obligors of the purchased receivables of the sale.

---

72. *See* Home Bond Co. v. McChesney, 239 U.S. 568 (1916); Dorothy v. Commonwealth Commercial Co., 116 N.E. 143 (Ill. 1917).
73. One interesting discussion of this question occurs in the British case, Lloyds & Scottish Fin. Ltd. v. Cyril Lord Carpets Sales Ltd., H.L. (Mar. 29, 1979) (transcript available on LEXIS).
74. People v. Service Inst., Inc., 421 N.Y.S.2d 325 (Sup. Ct. 1979).

In practice, the originator often is appointed as the collection agent initially. That is not necessarily inconsistent with characterization as a sale if (1) the originator, as collection agent, will be acting as an agent for the SPV pursuant to established standards, much like any other agent; (2) the originator will receive a collection agent fee that represents an arm's-length fee for those services; and (3) the SPV has the right at any time to appoint itself or another person as collection agent in place of the originator.

Sometimes collections of the purchased receivables are paid to the originator and commingled, or mixed, with the originator's general funds. That frequently occurs when the originator collects the receivables each day, but only remits the collections periodically (e.g., monthly) to the SPV. Besides raising a potential perfection question under the UCC,[75] commingling would, if permitted by the SPV, appear to be inconsistent with the concept of a sale: the originator would be using collections that belong to the SPV. That inconsistency often can be addressed by the originator's segregating and holding the collections in trust, pending remittance to the SPV or periodic reinvestment.

Additional Factors

The courts have identified a variety of other factors that do not fall within the categories discussed in the preceding section, but that may be indicative of a secured loan.[76] Among the more significant of these factors are the following:

1. The originator of receivables is a debtor of the SPV on or before the purchase date;
2. The SPV's rights in the receivables can be extinguished by payments or repurchases by the originator or by payments from sources other than collections on receivables;
3. The originator is obligated to pay the SPV's costs (including attorneys' fees) incurred in collecting delinquent or uncollectible receivables;

---

75. *See* page 40.
76. *See* WEIL, *supra* note 64, at 23–37.

Asset Securitization

4. The language of the documentation contains references to the transfer's being "security for" a debt; and
5. The parties' intent, as evidenced by the documentation and their actions, suggests that the parties view the transaction as a security device. Also of importance is how the parties account for the transactions on their books, records, and tax returns.

It is rare in modern commercial transactions for all the factors favoring a true bankruptcy sale to be met. There is inevitably a question of balance. Some recourse is needed to give a reasonable assurance to holders of the SPV's securities that they will be paid. It may be uneconomic for an originator to agree that the SPV obtains the entire surplus of collections once holders of the SPV's securities are paid. In each case, the parties structuring the transaction will have to balance how important it is that the transaction be a bankruptcy sale with the other commercial desires of the investors and the originator. The balance will depend, in large part, on the credit quality of the originator. It may be less important to investors to insist on a true sale for bankruptcy purposes where the originator has an investment-grade rating than where the originator is troubled or in a workout.[77] Of course, the FINCO, or two-tiered, structure often is the best practical solution for less-than-investment grade originators.[78]

Protecting Against the Fraudulent Conveyance Risk

An issue that sometimes arises is whether the transfer of receivables can be voided as a "fraudulent conveyance." The purpose of fraudulent conveyance law is to invalidate transfers made by a debtor

---

77. An originator sometimes may require that the receivables transfer be a loan for tax purposes so as, for example, to avoid recognition of a taxable gain that would be triggered if the transfer were treated as a tax sale. Because the bankruptcy and tax sale criteria, although not identical, are similar — and the bankruptcy courts may apply even closer scrutiny than the IRS — structuring a receivables transfer as a bankruptcy sale may well make it also a tax sale.
78. *See* discussion on pages 21–23.

Structured Finance

with the (actual or constructive) intention to "hinder, delay or defraud" creditors.[79]

Perhaps the most obvious situation in which a fraudulent conveyance risk would arise is where the SPV pays a purchase price that is less than the "reasonably equivalent value" of the receivables. The risk is minimal, however, in the typical structured financing, because the purchase price for the receivables normally will be determined on an arm's-length basis (although the fairness of the purchase price might be subject to greater scrutiny if the originator is a troubled company).

Even in a FINCO structure, where receivables may be transferred to a bankruptcy-remote subsidiary of the originator as a capital contribution, those transfers generally should not constitute fraudulent conveyances. It has long been held, for example, that parent support of a solvent subsidiary creates little chance of overreaching by the subsidiary, and ultimately inures to the benefit of the parent.[80] Nonetheless, capital contributions to companies that are not directly or indirectly majority-owned by the originator, or that are insolvent, would be subject to closer scrutiny by the courts.[81]

---

79. The sources of fraudulent conveyance law are federal (Bankruptcy Code § 548) and state. State fraudulent conveyance laws are based on either the recently promulgated Uniform Fraudulent Transfer Act, the predecessor Uniform Fraudulent Conveyance Act, or the 16th century Statute of Elizabeth in England. For a discussion of fraudulent conveyance law, see Schwarcz, *The Impact of Fraudulent Conveyance Law on Future Advances Supported by Upstream Guaranties and Security Interests*, 9 CARDOZO L. REV. 727 (1987); Schwarcz & Varges, *supra* note 20, at § 16.02(3)(c).
80. *See, e.g.*, Chester Airport, Inc. v. Aeroflex Corp., 237 N.Y.S.2d 752, 755 (Sup. Ct. 1962), *modified*, 238 N.Y.S.2d 715 (App. Div. 1963) (granting credit to a 51 percent subsidiary inherently brings benefit to the parent).
81. *See* Schwarcz & Varges, *supra* note 20, at § 16.02(3). For a discussion of these issues in the context of legal opinions, see Special Report by the TriBar Opinion Committee, *supra* note 28.

Asset Securitization

Additional Steps Required Under the UCC to Protect the Transfer

Once the SPV has been created and the transaction structured, it still will be necessary to take certain steps to protect the transfer of receivables against claims of third parties and in bankruptcy. The UCC, adopted (with only minor variation) in every state of the United States,[82] provides in section 9-102 that each transfer of an interest in "accounts" and "chattel paper," whether or not intended as a transfer for security or a transfer of actual ownership, must be perfected by one of the procedures set forth in the UCC (usually by the filing of a UCC-1 financing statement).[83] The commentary to section 9-102 (Official Comment No. 2) explains that the drafters had difficulty trying to set guidelines on whether a given transfer was a sale or a secured loan, and therefore established the same filing requirement in both cases. The purpose of the filing is to place third parties on notice of the transfer of the interest in the receivables, so they will not be misled when extending credit to or otherwise dealing with the originator. Any argument that the filing of UCC-1 financing statements indicates the parties' intention that the transaction constitute a secured loan and not a sale can be obviated by stating on the financing statement that the intention is to create a sale and that the filing is being made because the UCC requires it.

Perfecting the Transfer

The failure to perfect, in accordance with the requirements of the UCC, can have serious consequences. The secured party or purchaser

---

82. Louisiana has not adopted the Uniform Commercial Code as such. However, articles 1, 3, 4, 5, 7, and 8 of the UCC have been adopted in substance as LA. REV. STAT. ANN. tit. 10, ch. 1, 3, 4, 5 (West 1988) (commercial laws) under Act No. 92 of 1974 (effective Jan. 1, 1975), Acts No. 164 and 165 of 1978 (effective Jan. 1, 1979). Article 9 was adopted by Act No. 528 of 1988. U.C.C. Rep. Serv. (Callaghan), State Correlation Tables, Louisiana (1989).
83. Chattel paper, however, also can be perfected by the secured party's or buyer's taking possession of the collateral. U.C.C. § 9-305. Sometimes possession may be a more desirable means of perfection for chattel paper. *Cf.* U.C.C. § 9-308.

Structured Finance

might not be able to enforce its rights, for example, as against later secured creditors who file financing statements covering the same receivables or as against the originator's trustee in bankruptcy.[84]

Curiously, although section 9-102 of the UCC refers to transfers of "accounts" and "chattel paper," it does not refer to, and therefore by its terms would not appear to apply to, sales of other types of payment streams. "Account" is defined in UCC section 9-106 as "any right to payment for goods sold or leased or for services rendered which is not evidenced by an instrument or chattel paper, whether or not it has been earned by performance." "Chattel paper" is defined in UCC section 9-105(1)(b) as follows:

> "Chattel paper" means a writing or writings which evidence both a monetary obligation and a security interest in or a lease of specific goods, but a charter or other contract involving the use or hire of a vessel is not chattel paper. When a transaction is evidenced both by such a security agreement or a lease and by an instrument or a series of instruments, the group of writings taken together constitutes chattel paper.

Many common types of payment streams, such as fees payable under a franchise contract, may not fall into either of those categories. Indeed, the UCC has other categories, including a catch-all category of "general intangibles," into which any payment stream falls that is not included in a specific category.[85]

Does the failure of UCC section 9-102 to refer to the sale of general intangibles mean that the drafters intended that no legal steps need be taken under the UCC to perfect such a sale, or does that failure mean that the UCC was not intended to vary whatever common-law requirements were applicable to sales of intangibles? The UCC is somewhat ambiguous.

The answer to that question, however, can have practical consequences. Prior to enactment of the UCC, different states had varying requirements as to how to protect the interest of a purchaser of ac-

---

84. *See* Bankruptcy Code § 544(a); *In re* Communications Co. of Am., 84 B.R. 822, 824 (Bankr. M.D. Fla. 1988); *In re* Kambourelis, 8 B.R. 138, 141 (Bankr. N.D.N.Y. 1981).
85. U.C.C. § 9-106.

Asset Securitization

counts receivable and other intangibles. One line of cases, followed in New York and various other states, provided that a sale is not perfected when the transferor retains "unfettered" dominion over collections.[86] A minority line of cases, following the English rule,[87] required notice to be given to the obligors on the receivables in order to perfect.

It is unclear, as a matter of law, whether those pre-UCC perfection requirements continue to apply to sales of intangibles that are neither accounts nor chattel paper under the UCC.[88] Such a result would create commercial confusion because of the varying and conflicting state requirements. Perhaps a better approach is to recognize that it is the universally followed procedure for anyone who extends secured credit or is concerned about collateral to search the UCC records. For example, if a company were merely to pledge, as opposed to selling, its intangibles, there is no question that the UCC, which by its terms covers the granting of a security interest in "general intangibles," would apply.[89] It therefore would appear illogical and inequitable for a buyer that has filed UCC-1 financing statements to be penalized because it did not also follow common-law perfection procedures that can be commercially impracticable in today's world. There are, however, few decided cases directly on point offering further guidance.[90]

Sometimes the payment stream sold will be evidenced by a promissory note or other negotiable writing evidencing an obligation to pay money. Under the UCC these are classified as "instruments" and, because they are negotiable, can only be perfected by the buyer's taking possession.[91]

---

86. *See* Benedict v. Ratner, 268 U.S. 353, 364–65 (1925).
87. Dearle v. Hall, 38 Eng. Rep. 475 (H.L. 1823, 1827); Corn Exch. Nat'l Bank & Trust Co. v. Klauder, 318 U.S. 434, 437 (1943).
88. Section 1-103 of the UCC states that principles of common law not inconsistent with the UCC will continue to apply. This is the so-called swiss cheese principle, because the common law fills the holes in the UCC cheese.
89. *See* U.C.C. § 9-102(1)(a).
90. *But see In re* Joseph Kanner Hat Co., 482 F.2d 937, 939 n.5 (2d Cir. 1973) (in the context of determining whether the assignment of a general intangible constituted a security interest or a "true sale," the court found that "[a]n outright sale of the claim would therefore not have been governed by the requirements of Article 9").
91. *See* U.C.C. §§ 9-105, 9-305.

Structured Finance

Commingling

A further concern arises under the UCC when the collections from the purchased receivables are not paid directly to the SPV, but instead are paid to the originator and commingled, or mixed, in accounts with the originator's general funds. UCC section 9-306(4) provides that in the event of the originator's "insolvency proceeding" (presumably meaning bankruptcy), collections of the receivables that are commingled at the time of a bankruptcy filing[92] may lose their perfected status and be subject to claims of other creditors and the trustee in bankruptcy.

In appropriate cases, particularly with financially weak originators, collections of receivables purchased by the SPV may be required to be paid by obligors directly to lockboxes and deposit accounts that do not contain the originator's general funds or, preferably, to lockboxes and deposit accounts owned and controlled by the SPV. The SPV also could enter into agreements giving it the right to take over the originator's lockboxes and deposit accounts under designated circumstances. Alternatively, if adequate arrangements cannot otherwise be established, an SPV may obtain the right to notify obligors to make payments directly to the SPV[93] and to "sweep" funds on a daily or other periodic basis from the originator's lockboxes and deposit accounts to accounts owned and controlled by the SPV.

Debtor-in-Possession (DIP) Securitization

Since 1990, securitization has even been applied to bankrupt companies. The first such transaction occurred in July of that year, when

---

92. Proceeds received by a debtor *after* its bankruptcy filings are not subject to a commingling risk because "Section 9-306(4) is per se inapplicable." *In re Bumper Sales, Inc.* (Unsecured Creditors' Comm. v. Marepcon Fin. Corp.), 20 Bankr. Ct. Dec. (CRR) 1212, 1216 (4th Cir. 1990). The court reasoned that section 9-306(4) of the UCC only applies to commingled proceeds up to and including the instant of commencement of the bankruptcy case.
93. An SPV may be reluctant, however, to give such a notice, and an obligor receiving such a notice may choose to ignore it until the obligor receives reasonable proof that the receivables have been sold. *See* U.C.C. § 9-318(3).

Asset Securitization

Allied Stores Corp., a chapter 11 debtor, securitized the private-label credit card receivables[94] of four of its bankrupt retail store subsidiaries. Although Allied was the first such DIP securitization,[95] its structure has been used as a model in several subsequent deals and therefore it remains instructive.

The Allied Stores securitization was structured in two steps. Allied Stores's retail subsidiaries first sold their receivables at a discount to Allied Stores Credit Corp. (Allied Credit), a finance company affiliate also in chapter 11, in a transaction recognized by the court as a "true sale" for bankruptcy purposes. Allied Credit in turn pledged those receivables and certain other assets as security for advances made by a newly created SPV, Mason Funding Corp.

Mason Funding was not affiliated with Allied Stores. It issued commercial paper in the public markets in order to raise the funds to advance to Allied Credit. The commercial paper was rated A-1+ by Standard & Poor's Corp. and P-1 by Moody's Investors Service, Inc., based not only on the quality of the receivables, but also on a 100 percent surety bond issued by FGIC (itself backed by a 15 percent letter of credit issued by a bank syndicate), and a 100 percent liquidity facility also provided by a bank syndicate (compare pages 13–15). The receivables sold to Allied Credit also were pledged as security for Allied Credit's obligations to reimburse the liquidity banks, Financial Guaranty Insurance Co., and the letter-of-credit banks. Any cash build-up from collection of the receivables purchased by Allied Credit (cash may build up because the receivables are purchased at a discount) effectively would be retained by Allied Credit as additional loss protection for the benefit of Mason Funding.

In its motion to the bankruptcy court for approval of the securitization facility, Allied Stores said that "some $10 million on an annu-

---

94. Private-label credit card receivables of a retail store are receivables owing by customers of the store on account of purchases of merchandise charged by customers to the store's own credit card. A Bloomingdale's credit card, for example, is a private-label credit card.

95. A chapter 11 debtor technically is referred to as a "debtor in possession" or (colloquially) a "DIP"; hence the term DIP securitization.

al basis" would be saved compared with the postpetition financing loan previously in place.[96]

There are, of course, certain possible risks with a bankrupt originator. For example, will the obligors on the receivables continue to make payments to a bankrupt company? If the receivables consist of short-term trade or retail credit card receivables, where the obligors already have received the goods to be sold or the services to be rendered and there are no apparent defenses to payment, then there is little reason to believe the obligors generally will not pay. This is especially the case where the originator is expected to continue operating in chapter 11 and the obligors wish to purchase additional goods or services. On the other hand, it is possible to take a more conservative approach. In the case of Allied Stores, for example, a satisfactory collection history in bankruptcy of approximately seven to eight months at the time of the securitization provided additional comfort that the retail credit card receivables would continue to be paid.

Another possible risk is whether the originator, if it acts as collection agent, will continue to have the ability and inclination to service and collect the receivables. Trade receivables, for the most part, would be expected to collect in the ordinary course without significant additional efforts. In the case of retail credit card receivables, Allied Stores also is instructive: although each retail store acted as its own collection agent, the majority of the receivables collected in the normal course through lockboxes, and there was an established collection infrastructure in place. In appropriate cases, of course, the parties can consider the back-up appointment of a substitute collection agent.

All this is further complicated by the possibility that an originator operating in bankruptcy as a chapter 11 debtor may, under certain

---

96. Motion of Debtors and Debtors in Possession for an Order Authorizing Allied Stores Credit Corp. to Obtain Secured Post-Petition Financing Pursuant to 11 U.S.C. § 364(c), Consol. Case No. 1-90-00130, at 3-4 (Bankr. S.D. Ohio June 29, 1990). By contrast, in subsequent DIP securitizations, Federated Department Stores said it would save approximately $15 million per year and Carter Hawley Hale Stores said it would save approximately $7.5 million per year.

Asset Securitization

circumstances, be liquidated. Although liquidation could, as a practical matter, create a further disincentive to an obligor's willingness to pay and could impair the originator's ability to pursue collections, liquidation of a company attempting to reorganize in chapter 11 is rare without the lead-time needed for the bankruptcy judge and various parties to become convinced that a reorganization will be unsuccessful. Particularly where the DIP securitization involves short-term receivables, there should be sufficient time for the facility to be paid out through collection of the receivables well before the originator itself goes into liquidation.

The unique advantage of bankruptcy, however, is that the structured financing needs court approval to be consummated. That provides an opportunity to try to obtain assurances from the court on such otherwise complex issues as whether the transfer of receivables from the originator to the SPV is a true sale for bankruptcy purposes (although, even if the transfer is not a true sale, the court may have the power to modify the automatic stay in bankruptcy to permit the exercise of remedies in default and to provide certain other assurances to a secured lender[97]), and whether the originator and the SPV can be substantively consolidated (see pages 24–26). The bankruptcy court order also may be able to provide that appropriate indemnity claims — perhaps even covering such matters as returns and other noncash adjustments (known as dilution) — are priority claims in bankruptcy.[98]

---

97. Indeed, in the case of Allied Stores, because the advance of funds by Mason Funding to Allied Credit was a loan and not a sale, the court ordered such assurances. *See* Order Authorizing Allied Stores Credit Corp. to Obtain Secured Post-Petition Financing Pursuant to 11 U.S.C. § 364(c), Consol. Case No. 1-90-00130, at ¶¶ 10, 12, 16 (Bankr. S.D. Ohio July 26, 1990). It should be noted, however, that even when a court modifies the automatic stay in bankruptcy to permit the exercise of remedies in default, the court could later decide to use its equitable powers to limit the exercise of remedies if necessary to prevent a liquidation of the debtor.

98. For a general discussion of bankruptcy, *see* Schwarcz, *Basics of Business Reorganization in Bankruptcy*, 68 J. COM. BANK LENDING 36 (1985), *revised and updated in* A SPECIAL COLLECTION FROM THE JOURNAL OF COMMERCIAL BANK LENDING: BANKRUPTCY 79 (1988). Also, for some additional background on DIP securitization, *see* Glover, *Structured Finance Goes Chapter 11: Asset Securitization by Reorganizing Companies*, 47 BUS. LAW. 611, 632–42 (1992).

Structured Finance

Many of the DIP securitization transactions completed to date have included 100 percent credit support from such third parties as FGIC and CapMAC. This is, of course, expensive. Recently, however, as illustrated by the case of P.A. Bergner & Co., securitization has been applied successfully to bankrupt companies without the need for third-party credit support.

In April 1992, Bergner and certain of its affiliates, all chapter 11 debtors, sold their private-label credit card receivables to a newly created bankruptcy-remote subsidiary, Great Lakes Credit Corp.[99] The commercial paper that Great Lakes issued to finance the purchase of the receivables received the highest ratings from Moody's Investors Service, Inc.; Duff and Phelps Credit Rating Co.; and Standard & Poor's Corp., despite there being no third-party credit support. Instead, the ratings were based on the high credit quality of the receivables, overcollateralization of approximately 21 percent, and additional credit support in the form of a $10 million reserve account (the facility itself being $225 million).[100]

The Bergner structure appears to be an efficient and effective way to accomplish DIP securitization transactions. In each case, however, questions will need to be addressed, such as whether the "advance

---

99. Motion for an Order Pursuant to (i) 11 U.S.C. §§ 105 and 363(b)(1) Authorizing Bergner Credit Corporation to Form and Capitalize Great Lakes Credit Corp., (ii) 11 U.S.C. § 363(b)(1) Authorizing P.A. Bergner & Co., CPS Dep't Stores, Inc. and Bergner Credit Corp. to Sell Receivables to Great Lakes Credit Corp. Pursuant to a Post-Petition Receivables Purchase Agreement and Related Agreements and (iii) 11 U.S.C. § 364 Approving Second Amendment to Revolving Credit and Guaranty Agreement, Consol. Case Nos. 91-05501 to 91-05516 inclusive, Case No. 91-05502, Case No. 91-05503, and Case No. 91-05504 (Bankr. E.D. Wis. Apr. 16, 1992).

100. A syndicate of banks also provided 100 percent liquidity support of the commercial paper. Advances by these banks, however, were intended only to protect against timing delays in applying collections of the receivables to payment of maturing commercial paper; and were not intended to protect against losses due to defaults on the receivables. If the securities issued by the SPV in Bergner were, for example, medium-term notes (maturing every two or three years) rather than commercial paper (maturing every month or period of months), presumably even the need for liquidity support would have been minimized.

Asset Securitization

rate" (i.e., the dollar amount raised compared with the amount of receivables and other assets that the originator must transfer to the SPV) is economically attractive.

Tax Issues

There are three central tax issues in structured finance transactions. The first issue is whether the transfer of receivables from the originator to the SPV will require the originator to recognize loss or gain for tax purposes. The second issue is the degree to which the SPV, as issuer of asset-backed securities, itself will be subject to tax (the so-called entity-level tax). The third issue is the tax treatment of investors in the securities issued by the SPV. The resolution of these issues depends in large measure on the structure of the particular transaction.

Transaction structures can be divided, from a tax standpoint, into three categories. If the SPV issues debt securities, backed by the receivables and giving holders of the securities a claim for periodic payments in amortization of their investment, the structure is referred to as a "pay-through." If the SPV, on the other hand, issues securities that represent an equity ownership in the receivables held in the SPV, entitling holders of the securities to be paid out of collections on the receivables, the structure is referred to as a "pass-through."[101] The third category, referred to as a "real estate mortgage investment conduit" (REMIC), is characterized by the SPV's holding real estate mortgage loans.[102] The tax treatment will vary depending

---

101. In a typical "pass-through" structure, the receivables are deposited into a trust. The receivables are then effectively sold to investors by issuance of pass-through certificates in the trust, each of which represents the right to a pro rata portion of the unpaid principal balance of the receivables and of monthly interest payments on that principal balance.
102. Industry representatives have called for extension of the REMIC provisions to cover assets besides mortgage loans. To date, however, no legislation has been introduced to that effect.

Structured Finance

upon whether the particular structure is a pay-through, a pass-through, or a REMIC.[103]

Taxation of the Originator

It can be critical to the originator whether the transfer of its receivables to the SPV will require the originator to recognize loss or gain, for tax purposes, on the receivables transferred.

The controlling issue is whether the transfer itself constitutes a tax sale of the receivables or, instead, will be viewed for tax purposes as a loan secured by the receivables.[104] Only in the case of a tax sale does the transfer result in a taxable event.

Characterization of a given transaction as a sale or secured loan for tax purposes depends on whether there has been an effective shift of the benefits and burdens of ownership of the receivables. The inquiry depends primarily on the degree of shifting of economic risk, although other, more formalistic factors can also be looked to. Factors that are relevant to sale or secured loan characterization include the following ("yes" answers to the factors are consistent with a tax sale):

1. Does the SPV pay a price reflecting a fixed amount of stated discount as opposed to receiving a yield that is not fixed, and does the price, but for the discount, reflect substantially the full face value of the receivables?
2. Does the originator retain no residual power of disposition of the receivables and no benefit of appreciation thereof?
3. Have the specific receivables being transferred been identified?
4. Does the SPV receive legal title to the receivables?

---

103. The following discussion addresses only federal, and not state or local, income taxes. State and local taxes vary among jurisdictions and must be addressed in any transaction.
104. *Cf.* pages 28–35 of this monograph, which discuss whether a given transfer of receivables constitutes a sale or loan for bankruptcy purposes. The factors relevant to a determination of a tax sale are similar, but not identical, to those relevant to determination of a bankruptcy sale.

Asset Securitization

5. Is the SPV entitled to be paid interest or finance charges on the underlying receivables?
6. Do the obligors on the receivables receive notice of the transfer?
7. Does the originator retain no liability for state intangibles tax on customer notes used as collateral, or for excise or similar taxes?
8. Has the originator shifted all risk to the SPV for collection activities?[105]

The originator's retention of administrative or servicing duties with respect to the receivables is not necessarily inconsistent with a tax sale.

Even if the transfer of receivables does constitute a tax sale, the originator still might be able to defer recognition of loss or gain, at least to some extent. In a pay-through FINCO[106] structure, for example, the originator could sell or contribute its receivables to the capital of a wholly owned, bankruptcy-remote subsidiary (SPV$_1$). SPV$_1$ then could transfer the receivables to a second bankruptcy-remote entity (SPV$_2$), not owned by the originator, in a transaction structured as an accounting sale but a tax loan. SPV$_2$ will be the issuer of securities to investors. Because SPV$_1$ is wholly owned by the originator, it and the originator can file consolidated returns for federal income tax purposes; and the transfer of receivables to SPV$_1$ is treated as a deferred intercompany transaction, gain or loss with respect to which will not be currently recognized.[107]

---

105. *See, e.g.,* Alworth-Washburn Co. v. Helvering, 67 F.2d 694 (D.C. Cir. 1933); Elmer v. Commissioner, 65 F.2d 568 (2d Cir. 1933); Yancy Bros. v. United States, 319 F. Supp. 441 (N.D. Ga. 1970); Mather v. Commissioner, 57 T.C. 666 (1972), *acq.* 1973-1 C.B. 1; Rev. Rul. 82-144, 1982-2 C.B. 34; Rev. Rul. 80-96, 1980-1 C.B. 317; Rev. Rul. 65-185, 1965-2 C.B. 153; Rev. Rul. 54-43, 1954-1 C.B. 19; Gen. Couns. Mem. 39,584 (Dec. 3, 1986); Priv. Ltr. Rul. 83-38-043 (June 17, 1983); Priv. Ltr. Rul. 81-36-037 (June 10, 1981); Priv. Ltr. Rul. 80-15-118 (Jan. 18, 1980); Priv. Ltr. Rul. 79-22-055 (Feb. 28, 1979); Priv. Ltr. Rul. 79-17-085 (Jan. 26, 1979).
106. *See* pages 21–23.
107. *See* Treas. Reg. §§ 1.1502-13, 1.1502-14. There may, however, be recognition of gain or loss for state or local income tax purposes if no combined reporting is permitted under such tax jurisdictions.

Structured Finance

If the transaction is structured as a pass-through, the receivables are effectively deemed sold for tax purposes from the originator to the investors. The investors, by virtue of receiving an interest in all payments on the receivables and being subject to credit risk, prepayment risk, and interest rate risk, are deemed to bear the risks and possess the benefits of ownership of the receivables.[108]

In a REMIC transaction, taxation of the originator is governed by specific statutory requirements.[109] The transfer of mortgages to the REMIC in exchange for interests in the REMIC does not, by itself, result in the recognition of gain or loss.[110] A REMIC, however, issues two types of interests: "regular" interests, which are essentially debt instruments backed by the mortgage pool,[111] and "residual" in-

---

108. *See, e.g.,* United Surgical Steel Co. v. Commissioner, 54 T.C. 1215 (1970), *acq.* 1971-2 C.B. 3; Town & Country Food Co. v. Commissioner, 51 T.C. 1049 (1969), *acq.* 1969-2 C.B. XXV. In addition, numerous internal memoranda and private letter rulings have been issued by the IRS that stand for the proposition that a transfer of receivables will be treated as a sale provided that the transferor has relinquished substantial incidents of ownership. *See, e.g.,* Gen. Couns. Mem. 39,584 (Dec. 3, 1986); Gen. Couns. Mem. 38,147 (Oct. 26, 1979); Gen. Couns. Mem. 37,848 (Feb. 5, 1979); Gen. Couns. Mem. 34,602 (Sept. 9, 1971); Priv. Ltr. Rul. 83-38-043 (June 17, 1983). In this connection, excessive recourse to the originator for losses is deemed inconsistent with the finding of a tax sale directly to the investors, whereas limited recourse to the originator, or third-party credit enhancement for an arm's-length fee, is not necessarily found inconsistent therewith. The IRS has indicated, for example, that a holdback reserve of 10 percent or less of the discounted purchase price is not inconsistent with a sale, at least if the holdback does not substantially exceed the percentage of historical losses relating to the transferred receivables. *See, e.g.,* Priv. Ltr. Rul. 78-48-081 (Sept. 1, 1978); Priv. Ltr. Rul. 78-20-017 (Feb. 15, 1978); Gen. Couns. Mem. 39,584 (Dec. 3, 1986). *See also* Federated Dep't Stores, Inc. v. Commissioner, 51 T.C. 500 (1968), *aff'd,* 426 F.2d 417 (6th Cir. 1970). *Cf.* Rev. Rul. 84-10, 1984-1 C.B. 155; Rev. Rul. 71-399, 1971-2 C.B. 433.
109. The discussion of REMICs that follows is a summary one, which should not be taken as a substitute for a more detailed analysis of the rather intricate REMIC rules contained in Code sections 860A–860G. In addition, some states have adopted REMIC provisions based on the federal statute. Each relevant state's provisions must be checked in connection with any given transaction.
110. I.R.C. § 860F(b)(1)(A) (West 1993).
111. One or more classes of "regular" REMICs can be issued and may be subordinated to each other. Interest can be fixed or, to the extent provided in the regulations,

terests, which represent an undivided equity or ownership interest in the mortgage pool.[112] As the regular or residual interests are sold to investors, the originator will be required to recognize gain or loss.[113]

Taxation of the SPV

The next tax issue is whether the SPV itself will be subject to taxation on the income it earns.

It is generally desirable to avoid taxation of the SPV, because the SPV does not have an external funding source to pay the tax. If the SPV issues equity-type securities, as in the pass-through structure, taxation of the SPV would reduce the return to the holders of the securities.[114] If, however, the SPV issues debt securities, as in the pay-through structure, the SPV may be able to offset all or a portion of its income against interest paid by the SPV on the debt securities, mitigating the effect of taxation at the SPV level.

In a pass-through transaction, to avoid taxation of the SPV, the SPV is typically structured as a nontaxable "grantor trust" under sections 671 through 679 of the Internal Revenue Code.[115] In order to ensure grantor trust status, the trustee of the trust should not have the power to purchase new receivables or (except for permitted substitution for defective receivables during an initial period) substitute receivables, nor should the trustee have the power to reinvest moneys

---

variable or based on a specific portion of interest and principal received by the REMIC with respect to its mortgages. I.R.C. § 860G(a)(1) (West 1993).

112. I.R.C. § 860G(a)(2) (West 1993). Only one class of residual interests may be issued, and the interests are subject to certain restrictions on transfer. *See* I.R.C. § 860D(a)(2), (a)(6) (West 1993).

113. Any inherent gain or loss on interests that are retained by the originator will be accrued, with respect to regular interests, on a constant interest basis and, with respect to residual interests, on a straight-line basis over the anticipated life of the REMIC. *See* I.R.C. § 860F(b)(1)(C) (West 1993).

114. Distributions to holders of the securities would be treated, from the standpoint of the SPV, as nondeductible distributions to equity holders.

115. Items of income and loss realized by such trusts are passed through to the grantor or creator thereof. I.R.C. § 671 (West 1993).

Structured Finance

held by the trust.[116] As a result, in pass-through structures the distribution of payments to holders of securities issued by the SPV will typically correspond to the collection schedule of the receivables. In addition, the trust generally can issue only one class of beneficial interests without jeopardizing grantor trust status, although two classes are permitted where the sole distinction between the classes is that payments with respect to one class are subordinate to payments with respect to the other.[117]

In a pay-through transaction, on the other hand, the SPV will not qualify as a nontaxable grantor trust, because the SPV is obligated actively to manage cash flows to ensure that its debt securities will be paid at their scheduled maturities. To avoid separate taxation of the SPV in a pay-through transaction, the SPV is, therefore, structured either as a single-purpose subsidiary of the originator or, sometimes, so as to qualify as a partnership for tax purposes. If the SPV is a subsidiary with which the originator files consolidated income tax returns, any tax liability of the SPV can be offset by losses of the originator or other members of the consolidated group.[118] If the SPV is treated as a partnership for tax purposes, it would not be subject to an entity-level tax.[119]

---

116. *See* Treas. Reg. §§ 301.7701-4(a), 301.7701-4(c); Rev. Rul. 78-149, 1978-1 C.B. 448. In practice, however, tax attorneys are effectively relaxing this requirement somewhat.
117. Treas. Reg. § 301.7701-4(c). The rationale for permitting this particular form of multiple classes is that its purpose is to facilitate direct investment in the assets of the trust. The senior class would be sold to investors, with the transferor of receivables to the trust retaining the subordinate class as a form of overcollateralization. In this connection, the Internal Revenue Service originally had indicated that a transfer of the subordinate class would eliminate grantor trust status. In a later published revenue ruling, however, the Service reversed its position, holding that both the senior and subordinate classes may be sold to investors. Rev. Rul. 92-32, 1992-18 I.R.B. (Apr. 17, 1992).
118. Further, dividend payments can be made tax-free to the originator, thus eliminating double taxation on the residual income remaining in the SPV after the SPV's securities are paid off. *See* Treas. Reg. §§ 1.1502-13, 1.1502-14.
119. In order for an SPV to qualify as a partnership for tax purposes, the SPV must lack at least two of the following characteristics: (1) continuity of life, (2) centraliza-

Asset Securitization

The SPV is not subject to taxation if it qualifies as a REMIC.[120] The SPV can be a corporation, trust, partnership, or simply a pool of assets that has elected REMIC status. To qualify as a REMIC, however, the SPV must keep its books on the calendar year, use the accrual method of accounting, and fulfill certain other requirements relating to the types of assets it holds.[121]

---

tion of management, (3) limited liability, and (4) free transferability. *See* Treas. Reg. § 301.7701-2. Thus, a typical pay-through structure is a so-called owner trust that provides for the owners to retain management control (leaving a trustee with only ministerial duties), for joint and several personal liability of owners for expenses of the trust (other than payment on the securities issued by the trust), and for a requirement of consent to any transfer by an owner of its interest in the trust by other trust owners and the trustee. (Eliminating continuity of life is difficult to achieve with a trust, but is not essential because, as noted in the preceding section, it is only necessary to lack two of the four listed characteristics.)

120. There are, however, 100 percent taxes on (1) certain contributions to the REMIC after the start-up day; (2) certain net income from foreclosure property; and (3) income from "prohibited transactions," including nonpermitted dispositions of qualified mortgages, income on nonpermitted assets, income from performance of services, and certain income of cash-flow investments. *See* I.R.C. §§ 860F(a), 860G(c), (d) (West 1993).

121. *See* I.R.C. § 860D(a) (West 1993). In particular, substantially all of the REMIC's assets must, as of the close of the third calendar month beginning after the "start-up" day (generally the date of issuance of interests in the REMIC) and at all times thereafter, be "qualified mortgages" or "permitted investments." *Id.* "Qualified mortgages" are obligations, principally secured by real property (including residential, commercial, and co-op apartments and certain mobile homes), that are transferred to the REMIC on the start-up day or purchased, pursuant to a fixed-price contract, within three months thereafter. "Qualified mortgages" also include stripped interests, pass-through certificates, "regular interests" in other REMICs, and "qualified replacement mortgages" (defined as any mortgages substituted within three months of the start-up date or mortgages substituted for defective obligations within two years of the start-up date). "Permitted investments" consist of passive investments that mature on or prior to distribution dates on the REMIC's regular interests, certain assets held as part of a reserve fund (the size of which is subject to certain limitations and required reductions), and property taken in foreclosure, which generally may be held for only two years. I.R.C. § 860G(a) (West 1993).

Structured Finance

Taxation of the Investors

The last issue is how the holders of securities issued by the SPV will be taxed on their gain on the investment in such securities.

If the securities are debt securities, as in a pay-through structure, the holders of the securities will be taxed like any other holders of debt. Interest paid on the securities will be treated as ordinary income. Payment of principal generally will be nontaxable. If, however, there is original issue discount (OID), market discount, or short-term acquisition discount,[122] ordinary income will be reportable in amounts in excess of stated interest, and some payments of principal will be treated for tax purposes as taxable payments of discount.

If, on the other hand, the securities issued by the SPV represent an ownership interest in the receivables, the holders will account for their shares of the SPV's items of income and loss. Accordingly, they will treat principal payments with respect to the receivables as a nontaxable return of basis and must report all items of interest, OID, market discount, and short-term acquisition discount with respect to the receivables as ordinary income under their own methods of accounting.[123]

In a REMIC, the holders of "regular interests" are treated in effect as the creditors of the REMIC. They therefore must include, as ordinary income, interest and any OID or market discount to which they are entitled, which amounts must be reported under the accrual meth-

---

122. OID, market discount, and short-term acquisition discount relate to issuance or acquisition of receivables at a price less than their unpaid principal amount. The difference between principal amount and issue or acquisition price is, under certain provisions of the Internal Revenue Code, treated as equivalent to interest and taxed as ordinary income. A detailed discussion of these rules, which do not apply uniquely to structured finance transactions, is beyond the scope of this monograph.
123. Any tax basis remaining following prepayment or final payment of the receivable will generate a loss, and any excess of principal received over tax basis will generate a gain. Such gain, except to the extent of remaining OID, market discount, or short-term acquisition discount, will generally be capital gain to the holder if the obligor is not an individual and if the beneficial interest is a capital asset of the holder. *See* I.R.C. § 1271(a) (West 1993).

Asset Securitization

od of accounting.[124] The REMIC's "residual interest" holders, on the other hand, are effectively the owners of the mortgages. They therefore must take into account, in any taxable year, the taxable income or loss of the REMIC for that portion of the year during which they hold their REMIC interest.[125]

Regulatory Requirements

In structuring an asset-securitization transaction, one must take into account a number of federal and state regulatory requirements. The issuance of securities by the SPV, as well as an originator's transfer of receivables to the SPV, may raise the issue of whether registration under the Securities Act of 1933 (the 1933 Act)[126] and state "blue-sky" laws is required and whether, as a result of such issuance and transfer, the SPV inadvertently has become an "investment company" within the meaning of the Investment Company Act of 1940 (the 1940 Act).[127] Moreover, there might be special concerns

---

124. I.R.C. § 860B (West 1993). In addition, any gain on sale of a regular interest is treated as ordinary income to the extent that a prescribed rate of return exceeds any previously reported ordinary income. *Id.*
125. *See* I.R.C. § 860C (West 1993). In no event, however, may the holder of a residual interest (except for certain financial institutions) report as income less than the "excess inclusion" with respect to such interest for such year. *See* I.R.C. § 860E(a) (West 1993). This "excess inclusion" constitutes the excess of REMIC taxable income over the product of a prescribed interest rate and the REMIC's adjusted basis in the residual, or, if the residual is not significant, the entire REMIC taxable income. *See* I.R.C. § 860E(c) (West 1993). The excess inclusion is taxable as "unrelated business taxable income" to pension plans and other tax-exempt entities (I.R.C. § 860E[b] [West 1993]), and is subject to withholding tax upon distribution to non-United States persons, without reductions by treaty. I.R.C. § 860G(b) (West 1993). A residual interest holder's basis in the REMIC is increased by the holder's share of REMIC income and decreased by the share of REMIC losses and by distributions. *See* I.R.C. § 860C(d) (West 1993).
126. Pub. L. No. 22, ch. 38, 48 Stat. 74 (codified as amended at 15 U.S.C. §§ 77a *et seq.*). The 1933 Act is hereinafter cited to the appropriate section as amended.
127. Pub. L. No. 768, ch. 686, 54 Stat. 789 (codified as amended at 15 U.S.C. §§ 80a *et seq.*). The 1940 Act is hereinafter cited to the appropriate section as amended.

(discussed in the following) if the originator is itself a regulated industry or financial institution.

Investment Company Act of 1940

Turning first to the investment company issue, the 1940 Act provides that any entity principally engaged in owning or holding "securities" must, subject to certain exemptions, register with the Securities and Exchange Commission (SEC) as an investment company.[128] The 1940 Act was promulgated as part of the comprehensive federal securities legislation enacted through the 1930s to curb a number of perceived abuses in the United States securities markets, to protect the public from being defrauded, and to ensure adequate controls and information. Unlike the 1933 Act and the non-broker-dealer sections of the Securities Exchange Act of 1934 (the 1934 Act),[129] which focus principally on the adequacy of disclosure in connection with the issuance, sale, and trading of securities, the 1940 Act is a comprehensive, *substantive* regulatory scheme. Compliance with the 1940 Act is usually very costly and burdensome.[130] Accordingly, registration of an SPV as an investment company is generally considered infeasible, and transactions are structured so as to fall

---

128. One can perhaps intuitively understand the purpose behind the 1940 Act if one views a company that is principally engaged in owning or holding securities as a miniature stock exchange, and investors in the company as investors in stock traded on the exchange.
129. Pub. L. No. 291, 48 Stat. 881 (codified as amended at 15 U.S.C. §§ 78a *et seq.*). The 1934 Act is hereinafter cited to the appropriate section as amended.
130. For example, the 1940 Act imposes the following general requirements on registered investment companies:
   1. restrictions on capital structure (e.g., prohibitions or restrictions on the issuance of debt securities) in section 18;
   2. restrictions on the composition of the board of directors or other governing body (e.g., limits on the number of "interested persons" appointed) in sections 10 and 16;
   3. restrictions on investment activities (e.g., limits on investments in other investment companies) in section 12(d) and (e);
   4. regulation of advertising (e.g., filing of sales literature with the SEC) in section 24(b);

Asset Securitization

within various statutory and regulatory exemptions from 1940 Act registration.

Under section 3(a) of the 1940 Act, an investment company is defined in relevant part as (1) an entity that is "engaged primarily ... in the business of investing, reinvesting, or trading in securities" or (2) an entity, "engaged" in such business, that "owns or proposes to acquire investment securities having a value exceeding 40 per centum of the value of such [entity's] total assets (exclusive of Government securities and cash items) on an unconsolidated basis." The term "security" is defined broadly under section 2(a)(36) of the 1940 Act to include notes, stocks, bonds, evidences of indebtedness, transferable shares, investment contracts, and "any interest or instrument commonly known as a 'security.'"[131]

Most receivables and payment streams appear to fall within the definition of the term "security" under the 1940 Act, because they are "evidences of indebtedness." Nevertheless, several effective exemptions from registration as an investment company may be available to an SPV. Although various legislative and regulatory changes to the 1940 Act have been proposed, including the recently adopted rule 3a-7, discussed below, one of the most frequently used exemptions until recently had been section 3(c)(5)(A) of the 1940 Act. That section excludes from the definition of "investment company" entities that are "primarily engaged" in acquiring or holding receivables that constitute "notes, drafts, acceptances, open accounts receivables, and

---

5. required shareholder votes on a number of issues (e.g., approval of advisers' contracts, changes in investment policies, and appointment of auditors) in sections 13, 15(d), and 31;
6. ongoing reporting and disclosure requirements in sections 29 and 30; and
7. extensive and complicated controls on pricing of investment company shares in section 22.

131. Under section 3(a), the term "investment securities" is defined to include all securities except government securities, securities issued by employees' securities companies, and securities issued by majority-held subsidiaries (provided the owner is not itself an investment company).

Structured Finance

other obligations representing part or all of the sales price of merchandise, insurance, and services."[132]

Many, but not all, types of receivables will fall under the section 3(c)(5)(A) exclusion. These will generally include the most commonplace type of receivable — trade accounts receivable — since they clearly constitute the purchase price of merchandise.[133] Other types of receivables might not, however, come clearly within the section 3(c)(5)(A) exclusion.[134] In some of those instances, however, it has been possible to obtain a "no-action" letter[135] from the SEC, which will in practice have basically the same effect as an exemption from investment company registration.

In the Days Inn of America, Inc. letter,[136] for example, the SEC staff stated that it would not recommend enforcement action under

---

132. *Id.* Section 3(c)(5)(B) similarly exempts entities primarily engaged in making loans to manufacturers, wholesalers, retailers, and prospective purchasers of "specific merchandise, insurance, and services." Under section 3(c)(5)(C), entities primarily engaged in "purchasing or otherwise acquiring mortgages and other liens on and interests in real estate" are also excluded from the definition of "investment company" under the 1940 Act. It is that latter exemptive provision that originally was used in securitizing mortgage loans.
133. 1940 Act § 3(c)(5)(A) (sales price of merchandise).
134. The SEC has repeatedly emphasized the legislative history of section 3(c)(5)(A), (B) (originally 1940 Act § 3[c][6][A], [B], 54 Stat. at 798–99), which indicates that those subsections were intended to exclude sales finance companies, factoring companies, and similar entities from the scope of the 1940 Act. In the case of section 3(c)(5)(B), the SEC staff has interpreted that exemption somewhat narrowly and has refused, for example, to issue no-action letters to companies engaged in making general working capital loans. *See, e.g.*, Alleco, Inc., SEC No-Action Letter, Ref. No. 88-165 (July 14, 1988), LEXIS, FEDSEC library, No-Act file (section 3[c][5][B] does not include "a loan that does not relate to the purchase price of specific goods or services even if the loan is secured by the same kind of collateral that secures a sales financing loan"). In an attempt to reduce reliance on section 3(c)(5) by issuers in structured finance transactions, in November 1992 the SEC adopted a new rule under the 1940 Act, rule 3a-7, to exempt structured financings meeting certain criteria from compliance therewith (see the discussion on pages 58–61).
135. A "no-action" letter is a nonbinding response by the SEC staff to a private inquiry indicating that the staff of the SEC will not recommend to the SEC that any enforcement action be taken if a proposed transaction is carried out in a specific manner.

Asset Securitization

section 3(c)(5)(A) if a wholly owned subsidiary of Days Inn acquired certain franchise fee receivables from Days Inn (through another subsidiary), privately issued and sold notes secured by those receivables, and lent the net proceeds from the note sales to Days Inn to refinance certain indebtedness of the parent company. The receivables were characterized as obligations representing part or all of the sales price of various services rendered by Days Inn to its franchisees, and on that basis were found to fall within the scope of section 3(c)(5)(A).[137]

If section 3(c)(5) does not cover the receivables in question, other exemptions may be available. Under section 3(c)(1) of the 1940 Act, for example, "[a]ny issuer whose outstanding securities (other than short-term paper) are beneficially owned by not more than one hundred persons and which is not making and does not presently propose to make a public offering of its securities" is excluded from the definition of "investment company." This so-called private investment company exemption is frequently used in conjunction with the private offering exemption under the 1933 Act (discussed below) to place interests in an SPV with a limited number of institutional investors and other holders.[138]

---

136. SEC No-Action Letter, Ref. No. 88-688-CC (Dec. 30, 1988) (LEXIS, FEDSEC library, No-Act file).

137. *See also* Ambassador Capital Corp., SEC No- Action Letter, Ref. No. 86-402-CC (Sept. 4, 1986) (LEXIS, FEDSEC library, No-Act file) (purchase of air travel credit card program accounts receivable falls within section 3[c][5][A]); Woodside Group, SEC No-Action Letter, Ref. No. 81-713-CC (Mar. 15, 1982) (LEXIS, FEDSEC library, No-Act file) (same result regarding acquisition of equipment/facilities lease purchase and option agreements).

138. In placing interests with institutional investors and other entities under the exemption for 100 persons or fewer set forth in section 3(c)(1), care must be taken to comply with the rule for determining beneficial ownership under section 3(c)(1)(A). Pursuant to that subsection, beneficial ownership by a company is generally deemed to be ownership by only one person. In an important exception to that general rule, however, it is necessary to look through the investing company and count its ultimate security holders if the company owns 10 percent or more of the outstanding securities of the SPV *unless* the value of all securities owned by such company in all issuers exempted under section 3(c)(1), together with all securities in issuers that would be exempt thereunder were it not for the beneficial

Structured Finance

If no statutory exemption is clearly available, sections 3(b)(2) and 6(c) of the 1940 Act permit an SPV to petition the SEC to issue an order exempting the SPV from registration on the grounds that either (1) the SPV is primarily engaged in a business other than that of investing, owning, or trading in securities (under section 3[b][2]) or (2) an exemption is necessary or appropriate in the public interest and is consistent with the protection of investors and the other purposes of the 1940 Act (under section 6[c]). Obtaining a decision on such an application can take several months, and certainly there is no guarantee that an exemptive order will ultimately be issued by the SEC. Nevertheless, there is sometimes no alternative if investment company registration is not cost-effective and another exemption cannot be found.

Recently, however, certain legislative and regulatory changes to the 1940 Act were proposed, and a new rule was adopted by the SEC, that will have a dramatic effect on the application of the 1940 Act to structured financings. In April 1992, legislation was introduced in the Senate[139] that proposed (1) to simplify the beneficial ownership provisions contained in section 3(c)(1) of the 1940 Act to broaden the scope of companies permitted to invest in an SPV otherwise exempt thereunder[140] and (2) to create an exemption from the definition of investment company for companies whose outstanding

---

ownership rules, does not exceed 10 percent of the investing company's total assets. However, on April 2, 1992, legislation was introduced in the Senate to, among other things, amend the beneficial ownership provisions of section 3(c)(1) to broaden the scope of investing companies permitted to purchase interests in an SPV. S. 2518, 102d Cong., 2d Sess., 138 CONG. REC. 49 (1992) (see the discussion in note 140 and accompanying text).

139. S. 2518, 102d Cong., 2d Sess., 138 CONG. REC. 49 (1992). On April 2, 1992, the Senate Committee on Banking, Housing and Urban Affairs proposed the Small Business Incentive Act of 1992. The intent of this legislation was to promote capital formation for small businesses and others through exempted offerings under the 1933 Act, through investment pools that are excepted or exempted from regulation under the 1940 Act, and through business development companies.

140. More specifically, ownership of an investing company must be examined only if the company owns 10 percent or more of the outstanding securities of the issuer *and* the investing company is, or but for the exceptions set forth in section 3(c)(1) or 3(c)(7) would be, an investment company.

Asset Securitization

securities are exclusively owned by persons deemed to be "qualified purchasers" (as determined by the SEC) at the time of purchase.[141] In addition, on November 19, 1992, the SEC adopted a new rule 3a-7 under the 1940 Act that excludes from the definition of investment company SPVs meeting certain criteria.[142] Concurrently with the adoption of rule 3a-7, the SEC confirmed that it would not pursue any legislative changes to section 3(c)(5) of the 1940 Act at that time.

Although rule 3a-7 was adopted only recently, it would appear that its impact on structured finance will be profound. The rule, effective immediately, is intended to exempt most structured financings from the definition of "investment company," and to "remove an unnecessary and unintended barrier to the use of structured financings in all sectors of the economy."[143] The rule essentially provides an exemption from the 1940 Act for structured financings consistent with the practice in today's capital markets, as opposed to earlier exemptions (such as section 3[c][5]) that relied on historically relevant differences in the nature of the receivables held by the SPV that are no longer meaningful.[144]

Rule 3a-7 provides, in essence, that an SPV that purchases or otherwise holds receivables (or other "financial assets" that, by their

---

141. "Qualified purchaser" was proposed to be defined as "any person whom the [SEC], by rule or regulation, has determined does not need the protections of [the 1940 Act]." The Senate also proposed that the SEC, in making that determination, be required to consider an investor's financial sophistication, net worth, knowledge of and experience in financial matters, amount of assets owned or under management, and relationship with the issuer.
142. SEC Investment Company Act Release No. 19,105 (Nov. 19, 1992) (codified at 17 C.F.R. § 270.3a-7) (issuers of asset-backed securities).
143. *Id.*
144. This is not to say, however, that section 3(c)(5) is no longer meaningful and should be changed. Because section 3(c)(5) heretofore has been the most relied-upon exemption, its longstanding use and the comfort that both representatives of industry and the regulators have had with it have made section 3(c)(5) into a meaningful exemption beyond its historical roots. Indeed, as discussed below, the SEC has decided not to pursue any legislative changes at this time to section 3(c)(5).

Structured Finance

terms, convert into cash within a finite time period[145]) will not be deemed to be an investment company if four conditions are met. The first condition is that the SPV issue securities whose payment depends primarily[146] on the cash flow from such receivables or other financial assets. The second condition is that, except as provided below, the securities being issued must be nonredeemable debt securities or equity securities with debt-like characteristics ("fixed-income securities"[147]) that, in each case, are rated, at the time of their initial sale, as investment-grade or better[148] by at least one nationally recognized rating agency. An exception to the second condition is that nonrated securities may be sold to "qualified institutional buyers"[149] and that nonrated fixed-income securities may be sold to "accredited investors,"[150] as those terms are defined in rules promulgated under the 1933 Act.

The third condition is that the SPV acquire or dispose of receivables or other financial assets only in accordance with the terms of the agreements pursuant to which the SPV's securities are issued, and not for the primary purpose of recognizing gains or decreasing losses resulting from market value changes; and that such acquisitions or dispositions not result in a downgrading of the rating on the securities. These conditions apparently are intended to discourage any misuse of the exemption to permit speculation and also to avoid portfolio management practices resembling those used by mutual funds.

---

145. The term "financial assets" is broad enough to include virtually any conceivable payment stream.
146. The term "primarily" was used to clarify that a portion of the cash flows used to pay the securities could come, for example, from such sources as the disposition of assets that do not conform to a representation or warranty, and that residual interests could be paid, in part, from proceeds of the disposition of assets. *See* SEC comments in Investment Company Act Release No. 19,105 nn.36, 37 and accompanying text.
147. Preferred stock, for example, would appear to constitute a type of fixed-income security.
148. That is, at least BBB- for long-term securities or the equivalent for short-term securities.
149. *See* note 160 and the discussion of rule 144A.
150. *See* note 158 and the discussion of regulation D.

Asset Securitization

The fourth, and final, condition is that if the SPV issues securities that are not exempt under section 3(a)(3) of the 1933 Act,[151] the SPV must appoint an independent trustee for those securities. The trustee must meet certain legal requirements referred to in the rule, and also is obligated to "take reasonable steps" to obtain a perfected security or ownership interest in the receivables or other financial assets that "principally generate the cash flow need to pay" the securities.[152] In addition, the trustee must take actions necessary for the collections on the receivables and other financial assets to be deposited *periodically* in a segregated account maintained or controlled by the trustee for the benefit of the securities holders, but the trustee need not prevent commingling of collections during the period of time before the collections are deposited. This represents a practical compromise by the SEC to protect the collections, but in a manner intended to be consistent with industry and rating agency practice.[153]

Securities Act of 1933 and Securities Exchange Act of 1934

Even if an SPV establishes an exemption from registration under the 1940 Act, it still will be subject to the 1933 Act and the 1934 Act to the extent that it issues nonexempt securities. The 1933 Act imposes standards of disclosure[154] and requires the filing of a registration statement with the SEC in connection with any public offering of nonexempt securities.[155] The 1934 Act also imposes liability for

---

151. *See* note 162 and accompanying text. This is the so-called commercial paper exemption.
152. Thus a perfected interest only has to be obtained in the primary cash flows and *not* in the underlying assets, such as automobiles that are the subject of securitized leases or loans. *See* SEC comments in Investment Company Act Release No. 19,105, note 146 *supra*, at n.82.
153. *See* SEC comments in *id.* at 26–28. The author questions, however, whether an independent trustee really is needed for the broad segment of the asset-backed securities market sold to institutional investors pursuant to the exemption available under section 4(2) of the 1933 Act.
154. 1933 Act §§ 7, 10.
155. 1933 Act § 5(c).

certain types of fraudulent statements or omissions and, for certain publicly held issuers, imposes ongoing reporting requirements.

In considering methods of compliance with the 1933 Act, various factors must be weighed. For example, if the receivables to be acquired by the SPV are highly predictable payment streams, the originator has at least several years of collection experience, and the anticipated financing is large enough to justify the registration and related costs, an SPV may well choose to file a registration statement with the SEC and issue its securities as part of a public offering. Although such a registration can take several months to implement and is costly, registered securities issued by an SPV have the advantage of being freely issuable to and traded by the public and therefore can be purchased by a wide range of investors.[156]

If a public market is impracticable or otherwise not appropriate, the SPV may choose instead to issue its securities in a private placement under section 4(2) of the 1933 Act, which exempts from registration "transactions by an issuer not involving any public offering." If the private placement is made to a relatively few large institutional investors, such as pension funds and banks, relatively little in the way of specialized disclosure documents may be required: such investors are generally presumed to have the sophistication and bargaining power to elicit from the issuer and its sponsors the financial and other information necessary to make an informed investment decision.

If the private placement is to a larger number of investors, and particularly if noninstitutional investors are involved, the SPV and its sponsors might find it prudent to comply with the "safe-harbor" provisions of regulation D promulgated by the SEC.[157] Under that rule, the SPV may, in general, sell its securities to up to thirty-five

---

156. Recently, however, form S-3 (the SEC's short registration form) under the 1933 Act was revised to expand the benefit of rule 415 (the so-called shelf-registration rule) to offerings of investment-grade asset-backed securities. *See Simplification of Registration Procedures for Primary Securities Offerings,* Securities Act Release No. 6,964 (Oct. 22, 1992), 57 Fed. Reg. 48,970 (Oct. 29, 1992), to be codified at 17 C.F.R. pts. 230, 239, 240, 249.

157. 17 C.F.R. §§ 230.501-506 (1992).

Asset Securitization

"non-accredited" investors and an unlimited number of "accredited" investors.[158] If "non-accredited" investors are included, it will generally be necessary to prepare and circulate a private offering memorandum setting forth certain financial and other information required to be furnished under regulation D.

Regardless of whether the regulation D safe harbor is used, securities issued in a private placement will generally be deemed to be "restricted securities" and may not be resold except in compliance with the registration requirements of the 1933 Act or an exemption therefrom, such as SEC rule 144[159] or SEC rule 144A.[160]

Certain other exemptions may be available under the 1933 Act to an SPV that wishes to issue its securities in the public market, but wants to avoid the time and cost of filing a registration statement. If the securities are fully supported by a bank letter of credit, for example, the securities would be exempt from registration under section 3(a)(2) of the 1933 Act.[161] Under the more frequently used section

---

158. In addition to banks, insurance companies, and other institutional investors, the categories of accredited investors under regulation D include individuals with a net worth of $1 million or more and partnerships and corporations with total assets in excess of $5 million. 17 C.F.R. § 230.501(a)(5), (3) (1992).
159. 17 C.F.R. § 230.144 (1992). In general, that rule imposes a two-year holding period unless the securities are resold in another private transaction (in which case the securities will generally continue to be "restricted" in the hands of the buyer).
160. Rule 144A generally provides a nonexclusive "safe-harbor" exemption for specified resales of restricted securities to "qualified institutional buyers," provided that such buyers had more than $100 million in the aggregate owned and invested in securities on a discretionary basis (or $10 million in securities with respect to dealers). Securities Act Release No. 6,862. This rule is intended to increase the efficiency and liquidity of the private placement market. 53 Fed. Reg. 44,016 (1988), codified at 17 C.F.R. § 230.144A (1992).
161. Unlike section 4(2), which is a "transactional" exemption applicable to all types of securities, section 3 of the 1933 Act exempts entire specified classes of securities from the registration requirement of that act. Section 3(a)(2) included among those classes "securities . . . guaranteed by any bank," with the term "bank" defined to mean "any national bank, or banking institution organized under the laws of any State, territory, or the District of Columbia, the business of which is substantially confined to banking and is supervised by the State or territorial banking commission or similar official." That exemption is not often used in structured financings because the letter of credit typically covers only a portion of the securities.

Structured Finance

3(a)(3) "commercial paper exemption," securities having a maturity of no longer than nine months (i.e., 270 days), the proceeds of which are to be used for "current transactions," are also free from the registration requirements of the 1933 Act.[162]

In effect, the SEC has required that four criteria be satisfied in order for an issuance of commercial paper to qualify for the section 3(a)(3) exemption: such paper must (1) be of prime quality, (2) not be ordinarily purchased by the general public, (3) be used to facilitate current transactions, and (4) have a maturity of nine months or less with no automatic roll-over.[163] However, the most frequently encountered difficulty associated with the application of the section 3(a)(3) exemption is that the central requirement of a "current transaction" is not defined anywhere in the 1933 Act. The SEC has acknowledged that, with respect to financing companies (and by inference, with respect to SPVs), "current transactions . . . may properly include . . . the making of loans upon or the purchasing of . . . notes, installment contracts, or other evidences of indebtedness in the usual course of business."[164] However, to obtain more certainty

---

162. Specifically, section 3(a)(3) exempts

> [a]ny note, draft, bill of exchange, or banker's acceptance which arises out of a current transaction or the proceeds of which have been or are to be used for current transactions, and which has a maturity at the time of issuance of not exceeding nine months, exclusive of days of grace, or any renewal thereof the maturity of which is likewise limited.

The SEC, however, has adopted a more restrictive view of section 3(a)(3)'s application than a reading of the statute suggests on its face, stating:

> The legislative history of the [1933] Act makes clear that Section 3(a)(3) applies only to prime quality negotiable commercial paper of a type not ordinarily purchased by the general public, that is, paper issued to facilitate well recognized types of current operational business requirements and of a type eligible for discounting by Federal Reserve banks.

Securities Act Release No. 4,412 (Sept. 20, 1961).

Commercial paper may also be privately placed without registration under section 4(2) of the 1933 Act (discussed previously), but that approach is less common.

163. 3 LOUIS LOSS & JOEL SELIGMAN, SECURITIES REGULATION 1190 (3d ed. 1989).
164. Securities Act Release No. 401 (1935). In a 1961 release, the SEC added that "the current-transaction standard is not satisfied where the proceeds of exempt com-

Asset Securitization

as to whether a proposed transaction meets the current-transaction standard, it is often necessary to turn to various SEC no-action letters interpreting what is and is not a current transaction under various circumstances.[165] Generally, the current-transaction standard precludes the use of proceeds of commercial paper for permanent or fixed investments in such assets as land, buildings, or machinery; for the purchase of securities or other speculative assets; or for any fixed-capital purpose.[166] However, financing companies have been permitted to purchase or finance the following representative assets having terms not exceeding five years with the proceeds of section 3(a)(3) exempt commercial paper: consumer loans, short-term commercial loans, loans and financing leases for nonpermanent capital equipment, retail installment paper, accounts receivable and inventory loans, and home-improvement loan paper.[167] Given that the SEC has issued hundreds of no-action letters interpreting the current-transaction standard, and that in many cases those interpretations are in con-

---

mercial paper are used for the discharge of existing indebtedness unless such indebtedness is itself exempt under Section 3(a)(3)." Securities Act Release No. 4,412 (1961).

165. *See, e.g.,* Westinghouse Credit Corp., SEC No-Action Letter (Apr. 3, 1986) (LEXIS, FEDSEC library, No-Act file) (proceeds used for equipment financing, acquisition of personal property through foreclosure, short-term commercial loans, accounts receivable loans, inventory loans, and floor plan loans all constitute current transactions); Independence Bancorp, Inc., SEC No-Action Letter (Feb. 11, 1986) (LEXIS, FEDSEC library, No-Act file) (proceeds used for various transactions having maturities not exceeding five years all constitute current transactions); American Fletcher Mortgage Investors, SEC No-Action Letter (Mar. 2, 1971) (LEXIS, FEDSEC library, No-Act file) (construction mortgage loans and warehousing loans with commitments for permanent takeouts in three years constitute current transactions, but development mortgage loan maturing in five years or less does not).
166. *See* Securities Act Release No. 4,412 (1961); LOSS & SELIGMAN, *supra* note 163, at 1194–95. However, under certain circumstances, interim financing of permanent or fixed investments may be undertaken with the proceeds of section 3(a)(3) exempt commercial paper. *See, e.g.,* Southeast Banking Corp., 1989 SEC No-Action Letter LEXIS 1157 (Nov. 21, 1989) (permissible to finance initial or remaining short-term [generally, five-year] portion of certain loans and leases).
167. Southeast Banking Corp., *supra* note 166.

Structured Finance

flict or are not easily reconciled, a more detailed analysis of the current-transaction standard is beyond the scope of this monograph.

It also should be noted that, regardless of whether an SPV issues exempt securities or issues nonexempt securities in an exempt transaction or a registered public offering, the antifraud provisions of section 10(b) of the 1934 Act and rule 10b-5 promulgated by the SEC thereunder will apply. Accordingly, an SPV and its sponsors would be liable if, in connection with the issuance and sale of its securities, they employed "any device, scheme, or artifice to defraud" or if they made "any untrue statement of a material fact or [failed] . . . to state a material fact necessary in order to make the statements made, in the light of circumstances under which they were made, not misleading."[168]

Other Regulatory Requirements

If the originator transferring its receivables to the SPV is in a regulated industry or is a financial institution, the laws, rules, and regulations applicable to the originator also may apply to the SPV. In the case of a bank, for example, transferring its own assets to an SPV, or underwriting asset securitization for a third party, the Glass-Steagall Act (the Act)[169] may restrict the bank's actions. The Act was a response to widespread bank failures after the stock market crash of 1929, and was intended to protect banks from the risks of such investment banking activities as underwriting. The Act applies to all national banks and state banks that are members of the Federal Reserve System. The power of a bank to underwrite the sale of interests in securitized assets only recently has been resolved. In 1987, the Comptroller of the Currency had determined that the sale by Security Pacific National Bank of mortgage pass-through certificates, representing fractional undivided interests in a pool of Security Pacific's own mortgage loans, was not in violation of the prohibitions on bank

---

168. 1934 Act § 10(b); Rule 10b-5.
169. Banking Act of 1933, Pub. L. No. 73-66, ch. 89, 48 Stat. 162 (1933) (codified as amended in scattered sections of 12 U.S.C.) (commonly referred to as the Glass-Steagall Act).

underwriting contained in the Act. The Comptroller's rationale, however, was that the sale by a bank of its own assets was not "underwriting" of the type prohibited by the Act and represented nothing more than the sale of bank assets. The sale of certificates was simply a new way of performing a permitted bank activity or was authorized as an incidental bank power; that the assets were being sold through the mechanism of pooling did not change that essential nature.

The Comptroller's determination subsequently was challenged by the Securities Industry Association (SIA). In 1988, a federal district court judge rejected the Comptroller's position.[170] In September 1989, however, the Second Circuit reversed the district court's decision and decided in favor of the Comptroller's position.[171] The court reasoned that banking activities that are explicitly authorized by statute, and the exercise of "all such incidental powers as shall be necessary to carry on the business of banking," are permitted to banks notwithstanding that such activities may constitute underwriting or other investment banking activities.[172] The court followed another circuit in including in a bank's "incidental powers" any activity that is "convenient [and] useful in connection with the performance of one of the bank's established activities pursuant to its express powers."[173] The court held that Security Pacific's use of mortgage pass-through certificates was indeed "convenient [and] useful" in connection with its express power to sell its own mortgage loans.[174]

There had been speculation over how broadly the Second Circuit's opinion could be read and whether it would have application to bank underwriting of pooled assets originated by third parties.[175] The Fed-

---

170. Securities Indus. Ass'n v. Clarke, 703 F. Supp. 256 (S.D.N.Y. 1988).
171. *See* Securities Indus. Ass'n v. Clarke, 885 F.2d 1034 (2d Cir. 1989), *cert. denied*, 110 S. Ct. 1113 (1990).
172. Securities Indus. Ass'n v. Clarke, *supra* note 171, 885 F.2d at 1043 (quoting Glass-Steagall Act § 16, codified at 12 U.S.C. § 24).
173. *Id.* at 1044 (quoting Arnold Tours, Inc. v. Camp, 472 F.2d 427, 432 [1st Cir. 1972]).
174. *Id.* at 1049.
175. For example, because a bank has explicit power to buy a mortgage loan from a third party and subsequently sell it, could the bank buy mortgage loans with the intention of pooling them for securitization?

Structured Finance

eral Reserve Board more recently has expanded the ability of a bank to underwrite and deal, through nonbank subsidiaries (known as "section 20 subsidiaries" because they are created pursuant to powers found in section 20 of the Glass-Steagall Act[176]), in securities of an affiliated bank or nonbank so long as the securities are rated by an unaffiliated, nationally recognized rating agency. Thus, the section 20 subsidiary of a bank holding company can underwrite and deal in securities backed by mortgage and consumer receivables.[177] The Federal Reserve Board, however, has imposed an overall 10 percent limit on the amount of total revenue a section 20 subsidiary may earn from underwriting and dealing in such securities. In April 1990, the United States Court of Appeals for the District of Columbia Circuit barred the SIA from bringing suit against the Board of Governors of the Federal Reserve System on the basis that collateral estoppel precluded the SIA from relitigating the Act claims.[178]

Risk-Based Capital Requirements

Certain banks and similar financial institutions (called "Regulated Institutions" herein) are required to maintain certain minimum "capital-to-total asset" ratios and certain minimum "capital-to-risk-weighted asset" ratios pursuant to the regulatory guidelines applicable to them (the "Guidelines").[179] The financial consequences of a

---

176. Glass-Steagall Act § 20, 48 Stat. at 188 (codified as amended at 12 U.S.C. § 377).
177. The Federal Reserve Board originally had given section 20 subsidiaries the power to underwrite these types of securities backed by receivables originated by third parties. A later expansion of these powers allows section 20 subsidiaries to underwrite these types of securities backed by receivables originated by the bank or its affiliates. Board of Governors of the Federal Reserve System, Order Approving Modification to Section 20 Orders (Sept. 21, 1989).
178. Securities Indus. Ass'n v. Board of Governors, Fed. Reserve Sys., 900 F.2d 360 (D.C. Cir. 1990).
179. The Guidelines consist collectively of the following: 12 C.F.R. pt. 3, app. A (1992) (national banks); 12 C.F.R. pt. 208, apps. A, B (1992) (state banks that are members of the Federal Reserve System ["state member banks"]); 12 C.F.R. pt. 225, apps. A, B, D (1992) (bank holding companies); 12 C.F.R. pt. 325, apps. A,

Asset Securitization

Regulated Institution's participation in an asset securitization, whether as an originator of receivables, as a provider of liquidity or credit enhancement, or as an investor in the related securities, will depend, in part, on the Guidelines.[180] Because the Guidelines are complex and differ slightly for each type of Regulated Institution, a comprehensive discussion thereof is beyond the scope of this monograph. Although the application of the Guidelines should be considered on a case-by-case basis whenever a Regulated Institution is involved in an asset-securitization transaction, a general discussion of the Guidelines follows below.

The Guidelines Generally

As discussed above, Regulated Institutions are required to maintain certain minimum[181] ratios of their "capital" to both their "total assets" and their "risk-weighted assets." The Guidelines provide complicated instructions to calculate each of the elements of these ratios. "Capital," for instance, may have several different formulations, each of which is used for a different capital to total asset or risk-weighted-asset ratio.[182] Generally, each definition of capital in-

---

B (1992) (FDIC-insured state banks that are not members of the Federal Reserve System ["state non-member banks"]); and 12 C.F.R. pt. 567 (1992) (savings associations).

180. *See* T. Boemio & G. Edwards, *Asset Securitization: A Supervisory Perspective*, 75 FED. RESERVE BULL. 659 (Oct. 1989) (general discussion of interrelationship between Guidelines and asset securitization); J. Shenker & A. Colleta, *Asset Securitization: Evolution, Current Issues and New Frontiers*, 69 TEX. L. REV. 1369 (1991).

181. With respect to bank holding companies, for example, the Guidelines provide that these ratios are *just* minimums, and organizations whose operations involve or are exposed to high or inordinate degrees of risk will be expected to hold additional capital to compensate for these risks. 12 C.F.R. pt. 225, apps. A, B (1992).

182. With respect to state member banks and bank holding companies, for example, "capital" can take the form of "Tier 1 capital," "Tier 2 capital," "primary capital," and "total capital," each consisting of a different combination of assets. The "capital" to "total asset" ratios use the "Tier 1 capital," "primary capital," and "total capital" measures, whereas the risk-based ratios use the "Tier 1 capital" and "Tier

cludes a specific combination of certain of a Regulated Institution's common stock, preferred stock, related surplus, contingency and other financial reserves, allowances for loan or lease losses, minority interests in equity accounts of consolidated subsidiaries, and other financial instruments. In addition, capital is often reduced by any outstanding goodwill and by certain other applicable adjustments.

With respect to the capital-to-total-asset ratios, "total assets" are generally defined as a Regulated Institution's average total assets as reported on the institution's financial reports filed with its applicable regulatory body.[183] Assets that a Regulated Institution may want to securitize, such as its outstanding loans or credit card receivables, would be included among a Regulated Institution's total assets.[184]

The calculation of "risk-weighted assets" required for determining the risk-based capital ratio is, however, more complicated. The Guidelines provide a framework for calculating a Regulated Institution's risk-weighted assets that involves assigning its assets and certain off- balance-sheet items (e.g., letters of credit, guarantees, and commitments to lend or to purchase assets) to broad risk categories. Each category has been assigned a corresponding percentage factor intended to reflect the credit and other risks associated with it. A Regulated Institution's total risk-weighted assets are equal to the sum of the items in each risk category weighted according to the category's corresponding percentage.[185]

---

2 capital" measures. 12 C.F.R. pt. 208, apps. A, B (1992) (with respect to state member banks); 12 C.F.R. pt. 225, apps. A, B, D (1992) (with respect to bank holding companies).

183. For example, when calculating the total asset ratio for a national bank, total assets are (generally) "the average total assets figure required to be computed for and stated in a bank's most recent quarterly *Consolidated Report of Condition and Income* (Call Report)." 12 C.F.R. § 3.2(a) (1992).

184. Intangibles are sometimes deducted from the total asset calculation. *Cf.* 12 C.F.R. § 3.2(a) (1992) (with respect to national banks, total assets is reduced by "end-of-quarter intangible assets that are deducted from Tier 1 capital") *and* 12 C.F.R. pt. 225, app. B (with respect to the leverage measure applicable to bank holding companies, the amounts of intangible assets are considered in the review of an organization's capital condition, but are not automatically deducted from total assets directly).

Asset Securitization

The Effect of the Guidelines on an Originator of Receivables

Because a Regulated Institution is required to maintain capital against its assets pursuant to the Guidelines, such an institution can reduce its capital requirements by disposing of assets. An asset securitization is often an effective means of accomplishing this.[186] However, in structuring the asset securitization, the Regulated Institution must ensure that the disposition of receivables is treated as a sale, and not as a financing secured by the receivables. Pursuant to the Guidelines, only an asset sale will achieve a reduction in such an institution's capital requirements.

Whether the transfer of an asset by a nonbank entity will be accounted for as a sale or secured loan is governed by generally accepted accounting principles (GAAP). However, the accounting treatment of transfers by FDIC-insured financial institutions, such as national banks, state member banks, insured state nonmember banks, and savings associations, is governed by the instructions for the Commercial Bank Reports of Condition and Income (the Call Report Instructions) published by the Federal Financial Institutions Examination Council (FFIEC). The criteria for an asset sale under the Call Report Instructions are more stringent than the GAAP criteria.[187]

Transfers of assets involving no recourse to the transferor are treated under both sets of criteria as asset sales. Under GAAP, Statement of Financial Accounting Standards No. 77 would permit transfers of receivables with recourse to be considered asset sales if

---

185. *See, e.g.,* 12 C.F.R. pt. 225, app. A, attachment III, for a summary of risk categories and their respective risk weights with respect to bank holding companies.
186. *See, e.g.,* T. Boemio & G. Edwards, *supra* note 180, at 664. The use of asset securitizations by Regulated Institutions may also provide them with a low-cost source of funding. In addition, such an institution may be provided with a continuous source of fee income by servicing the receivables it originates and then securitizes.
187. Note, however, that some Regulated Institutions may be subject to GAAP in addition to the Call Report Instructions. Nonetheless, for purposes of calculating the risk-based capital ratio, the Guidelines require the Call Report Instructions standard to be used in determining whether there is a sale. *See, e.g.,* 12 C.F.R. pt. 225, app. A (1992) (with respect to bank holding companies).

Structured Finance

1. the transferor surrenders control of the future economic benefits relating to the receivables,
2. the transferor can reasonably estimate its recourse obligations, and
3. the transferee can only return receivables to the transferor pursuant to the recourse provisions.[188]

For a transfer with recourse of receivables to be considered an asset sale under the Call Report Instructions, however, much stricter requirements must be met.

The Call Report Instructions provide generally that transfers of assets may be reported as sales only if the transferor (1) retains no risk of loss resulting from any cause from the assets transferred *and* (2) has no obligation to any party for the payment of principal or interest for any cause on the assets transferred.[189] Recourse arrangements, or the retention by the transferor of a subordinated class of securities, for example, may constitute the retention of risk. Transactions by Regulated Institutions involving such arrangements, therefore, are likely to be deemed secured borrowings rather than asset sales.[190]

There are, however, several exceptions to the foregoing rule. If the transferor retains risk equal to a percentage of future losses, rather than a percentage of the assets themselves, only that portion of the assets transferred equal to the risk of loss is deemed to be a borrowing, and the remaining portion of the transferred assets will be per-

---

188. The estimated recourse obligation is then recorded as a direct liability on the transferor's books and attracts risk-based capital treatment accordingly. *Id. See also* 12 C.F.R. pt. 208, app. A (with respect to state member banks). *But see* FASB Technical Bulletin No. 85-2, *Collateralized Mortgage Obligations* (similar but stricter rules relating to such obligations).
189. *See* the definition of "Sales of Assets" in the Glossary to the Call Report Instructions. Also, note that the entire issue of recourse arrangements and their treatment for capital and other regulatory requirements is under consideration by the Federal Financial Institutions Examination Council (FFIEC), which promulgated the Call Report Instructions.
190. T. Boemio & G. Edwards, *supra* note 180, at 665. However, the Call Report Instructions provide that provisions permitting the return to the transferor of assets in violation of certain basic warranties (i.e., breach of transferor's representations, incomplete documentation, or fraud) would not preclude sale treatment.

Asset Securitization

mitted sale treatment.[191] The Call Report Instructions also provide that transfers of residential mortgage loan pools under the GNMA, FNMA, and FHLMC programs will be accorded sale treatment if the risk retained reflects actual loss experience.[192] In addition, transfers of residential loan pools with retained risk, to the extent not executed through a government agency program (i.e., "private sales"), may be treated as sales if the maximum contractual risk of loss retained by the transferor is less than the reasonably estimated probable loss related to the transferred assets.[193] Further, if the transferor effectively retains risk through the build-up of a "spread account," sales treatment is also likely.[194]

The Effect of the Guidelines on Providers of Credit Enhancement or Liquidity

A Regulated Institution providing credit enhancement or liquidity support to an asset securitization also may be subject to additional capital requirements, particularly depending on its capital-to-risk-weighted-asset ratio.[195]

---

191. *See* the definition of "Sales of Assets" in the Glossary to the Call Report Instructions.
192. *See* the definition of "Participations in Pools of Residential Mortgages" in the Glossary to the Call Report Instructions. *See also* T. Boemio & G. Edwards, *supra* note 180, at 665.
193. *See* the instructions to Schedule RC-L, Item 9(b)(1), of the Call Report Instructions. *See also* T. Boemio & G. Edwards, *supra* note 180, at 666.
194. This is a collateral account created by depositing the interest rate or finance charges on the receivables being transferred in excess of the interest rate payable on the securitized debt being issued. *See* T. Boemio & G. Edwards, *supra* note 180, at 666; *Capital Adequacy Guidelines*, 55 Fed. Reg. 42,022, 42,024 (1990).
195. One of the enunciated goals of the risk-based capital guidelines was to "factor off-balance sheet exposures into the assessment of capital adequacy." The Guidelines provide a complicated procedure for incorporating these off-balance-sheet items into the risk-based capital ratio. *See, e.g.,* 12 C.F.R. pt. 225, app. A (1992) (with respect to bank holding companies). The capital-to-total-asset ratios, however, do not incorporate off-balance-sheet items directly; instead, with respect to bank holding companies, for example, "[t]he Federal Reserve will review the relationship of all on- and off-balance-sheet risks to capital and will require those institu-

Structured Finance

The Guidelines provide that off-balance-sheet items, such as credit enhancement or liquidity, are included in measuring the risk-weighted-asset ratio pursuant to a complicated formula. Nonetheless, the amount of capital required usually is proportional to the *face amount* of an off-balance-sheet item multiplied by a "conversion factor."

Direct credit substitutes are assigned a 100 percent conversion factor (i.e., maximum risk-based capital must be maintained against them). These include guarantees, financial standby letters of credit,[196] and other equivalent irrevocable undertakings or surety arrangements that guarantee repayment of financial obligations. Also included in this category may be legally binding contractual obligations to purchase assets at a set price on a specified future date.

Transaction-related contingencies with original maturities exceeding one year[197] are assigned a 50 percent conversion factor. These include loan commitments,[198] bid bonds, other types of commitments

---

tions with high or inordinate levels of risk to hold additional [capital]." "Particularly close attention will be directed to risks associated with standby letters of credit and participation in joint venture activities." 12 C.F.R. pt. 225, app. B (1992).

196. Financial standby letters of credit are distinguishable from performance standby letters of credit (which are generally assigned a 50 percent conversion factor [see the discussion immediately below]) in that the former are irrevocable obligations to pay the beneficiary when the customer fails to repay an outstanding loan or debt instrument, whereas the latter are irrevocable obligations to pay the beneficiary when the customer fails to perform some other contractual nonfinancial obligation. *See, e.g.,* 12 C.F.R. pt. 225, app. A (with respect to bank holding companies).

197. Original maturity has been defined as "the length of time between the date the commitment is issued and the earliest date on which: (1) the [Regulated Institution] can, at its option, unconditionally (without cause) cancel the commitment and (2) the [Regulated Institution] is scheduled to (and as a normal practice actually does) review the facility to determine whether or not it should be extended." *See, e.g.,* 12 C.F.R. pt. 225, app. A (with respect to bank holding companies). *See also Questions and Interpretations Relating to the Implementation of the Risk-Based Capital Framework,* FED. BANKING L. REP. (CCH) ¶ 5404 (July 3, 1990), for further discussion of the meaning of "original maturity" and "evergreen commitments."

198. A "loan commitment" "involves an obligation (with or without a material adverse change or similar clause) of the [Regulated Institution] to fund its customer *in the*

Asset Securitization

(such as commitments to purchase loans, securities, or other assets, or to participate in loans or leases), performance standby letters of credit, performance bonds, and warranties.

Unused portions of such transaction-related contingencies with an original maturity of one year or less (or that are unconditionally cancelable at any time, provided a separate credit decision is made before each drawing under the facility) are assigned a zero percent conversion factor.

Maintaining capital represents a cost to a Regulated Institution. If such an institution contemplates providing credit enhancement or liquidity as part of an asset-securitization transaction, it may attempt to structure the credit enhancement or liquidity in a way that minimizes the capital requirements. However, the Guidelines with respect to off-balance-sheet items are sometimes ambiguous; and it is not always easy to estimate the capital requirements with certainty. Although not directly binding as law, a recent article[199] in the *Federal Reserve Bulletin* with respect to capital requirements in asset-securitization transactions provides significant additional guidance, and helps to clarify the distinction between certain obligations deemed to be direct credit substitutes (i.e., having a 100 percent conversion factor) and those deemed to be mere commitments (having a zero or 50 percent conversion factor [depending on the commitment's maturity]).[200]

---

normal course of business should the customer seek to draw down the commitment" (emphasis in original). 12 C.F.R. pt. 225, app. A (1992) (with respect to bank holding companies).

199. B. Kavanaugh et al., *Asset Backed Commercial Paper Programs*, 78 FED. RESERVE BULL. (Feb. 1992).

200. The authors found, for example, that irrevocable facilities obligating a Regulated Institution to purchase such assets at the price paid by the issuer, regardless of the actual losses incurred on the assets, should be deemed direct credit substitutes. However, such facilities (even if irrevocable) that incorporate an asset-quality test into the purchase price (e.g., excluding the purchase of defaulted receivables) can be deemed a commitment.

The Effect of the Guidelines on Investors in Structured Finance Transactions

The Guidelines also require that Regulated Institutions maintain capital of some form against assets acquired as investments. Pursuant to the Guidelines, the risk category associated with a particular asset determines the amount of capital, if any, required to be maintained against it.

The risk categories for asset-backed and mortgage-backed securities vary according to the obligor, the guarantor, and the type of collateral provided to the holders thereof. Unless the security meets certain criteria, it would be assigned to the 100 percent risk category.[201]

Because securities guaranteed or issued by United States governmental or government-sponsored agencies are assigned to low risk categories in recognition of their perceived low credit risk (the zero percent and 20 percent categories, respectively), certain mortgage-backed securities so guaranteed (and certain "privately issued" mortgage-backed securities meeting specified criteria) are placed in these advantageous risk categories as well.[202]

Conclusion

In summary, asset securitization has significant potential for enabling companies to obtain economically advantageous financing without necessarily increasing leverage. Parties wishing to take advantage of asset securitization, however, might encounter many complex legal pitfalls. A well-designed structured financing will minimize and avoid those pitfalls.

---

201. *See, e.g.*, 12 C.F.R. pt. 225, app. A (1992) (with respect to bank holding companies). *See generally* T. Boemio & G. Edwards, *supra* note 180, at 667–68.
202. *See, e.g.*, 12 C.F.R. pt. 225, app. A n.30, for a more comprehensive listing of United States governmental agencies (and a definition thereof).

Tables of Authorities

(References are to pages.)

CASES

Adana Mortgage Bankers, Inc., *In re*, 17
AIC Indus., *In re*, 30
Alworth-Washburn Co. v. Helvering, 47
Arnold Tours, Inc. v. Camp, 68
Aronson v. Lewis, 18
Augie/Restivo Baking Co., *In re*, 25

Bankers Trust Co. v. J.V. Dowler & Co., 18
Benedict v. Ratner, 39
Bumper Sales, Inc., *In re*, 40

Chemical Bank N.Y. Trust Co. v. Kheel, 25
Chester Airport, Inc. v. Aeroflex Corp., 36
Citibank, N.A. v. Data Lease Fin. Corp., 18
Colonial Realty Inv. Co., *In re*, 9
Comcoach Corp., *In re*, 29
Communications Co. of Am., *In re*, 38
Corn Exch. Nat'l Bank & Trust Co. v. Klauder, 39
Credit Lyonnais Bank v. Pathé Communications, 17–20

Days Inn of Am., Inc., *In re*, 10-13, 19-21
Dearle v. Hall, 39
Dorothy v. Commonwealth Commercial Co., 33

Tables of Authorities

Elmer v. Commissioner, 47
Empire Life Ins. Co. of Am. v. Valdak Corp., 18
Evergreen Valley Resort, Inc., *In re*, 32

Fallick v. Kehr, 17
Federated Dep't Stores, Inc. v. Commissioner, 48

Gerry v. Johnston, 8
Gilbert v. El Paso Co., 18
Grayson-Robinson Stores, Inc., *In re*, 8

Hecht v. Malley, 23
Heritage N. Dunlap Trust, *In re*, 23
Home Bond Co. v. McChesney, 33
Hurricane Elkhorn Coal Corp., *In re*, 32

In re AIC Indus., 30
In re Adana Mortgage Bankers, Inc., 17
In re Augie/Restivo Baking Co., 25
In re Bumper Sales, Inc., 40
In re Colonial Realty Inv. Co., 9
In re Comcoach Corp., 29
In re Communications Co. of Am., 38
In re Days Inn of Am., Inc., 10-13, 19-21
In re Evergreen Valley Resort, Inc., 32
In re Grayson-Robinson Stores, Inc., 8
In re Heritage N. Dunlap Trust, 23
In re Hurricane Elkhorn Coal Corp., 32
In re Ionosphere Clubs, Inc., 10
In re Joseph Kanner Hat Co., 39
In re Kambourelis, 38
In re Lionel Corp., 10-11
In re Manzey Land & Cattle Co., 25
In re Michigan Real Estate Ins. Trust, 23
In re Mosby, 23

Tables of Authorities

In re National Fin. Alternatives, Inc., 27
In re Nixon Mach. Co., 32
In re O.P. Held, Inc., 30
In re O.P.M. Leasing Servs., Inc., 8
In re P.A. Bergner & Co. Holding Co., 19, 44
In re Sea-Land Corp. Shareholders Litig., 18
In re Seatrade Corp., 25
In re Slab Fork Coal Co., 9
In re Snider Bros., 25–26
In re Streets & Beard Farm Partnership, 8
In re Sunberg, 9
In re Sweetwater, 29
In re Timbers of Inwood Forest Ass'n, 30
In re Tru Block Concrete Prods., Inc., 17, 23
In re Universal Clearing House Co., 23
In re Vecco Constr. Indus., 25
In re Weitzen, 17
Ionosphere Clubs, Inc., *In re*, 10
Isquith v. New York State Thruway Auth., 8

Joseph Kanner Hat Co., *In re*, 39

Kambourelis, *In re*, 38
Katz v. Oak Indus., 18

Lionel Corp., *In re*, 10-11
Lloyds & Scottish Fin. Ltd. v. Cyril Lord Carpets Sales Ltd., 33

Major's Furniture Mart, Inc. v. Castle Credit Corp., 31
Manzey Land & Cattle Co., *In re*, 25
Mather v. Commissioner, 47
Michigan Real Estate Ins. Trust, *In re*, 23
Mosby, *In re*, 23

Tables of Authorities

National Fin. Alternatives, Inc., *In re*, 27
Nixon Mach. Co., *In re*, 32

O.P. Held, Inc., *In re*, 30
O.P.M. Leasing Servs., Inc., *In re*, 8

P.A. Bergner & Co. Holding Co., *In re*, 19, 44
People v. Service Inst., Inc., 33
Pepper v. Litton, 18
Price v. Gurney, 16

Revlon, Inc. v. MacAndrews & Forbes Holdings, 18
Rosenthal Paper Co. v. National Folding Box & Paper Co., 8

Sampsell v. Imperial Paper & Color Corp., 25
Sea-Land Corp. Shareholders Litig., *In re*, 18
Seatrade Corp., *In re*, 25
Securities Indus. Ass'n v. Board of Governors, Fed. Reserve Sys., 68
Securities Indus. Ass'n v. Clarke (2d Cir.), 67-68
Securities Indus. Ass'n v. Clarke (S.D.N.Y.), 67
Slab Fork Coal Co., *In re*, 9
Snider Bros., *In re*, 25-26
Streets & Beard Farm Partnership, *In re*, 8
Sunberg, *In re*, 9
Sweetwater, *In re*, 29

Timbers of Inwood Forest Ass'n, *In re*, 30
Town & Country Food Co. v. Commissioner, 48-49
Tru Block Concrete Prods., Inc., *In re*, 17, 23

United Surgical Steel Co. v. Commissioner, 48-49
United Va. Bank v. Slab Fork Coal Co., 9
Universal Clearing House Co., *In re*, 23
Unsecured Creditors' Comm. v. Marepcon Fin. Corp., 40

Tables of Authorities

Vecco Constr. Indus., *In re*, 25

Weitzen, *In re*, 17

Yancy Bros. v. United States, 47

FEDERAL LEGISLATION

Bankruptcy Code (Title 11, U.S.C.)

SECTIONS	SECTIONS
101(8)(A)(v), 23	363(b), 10, 19
101(9)(A)(v), 23	363(b)(1), 10, 45
101(41), 23	363(e), 11
105, 45	364, 30, 45
109, 15, 23-24	364(c), 42-44
301, 16	364(d)(1), 30–31
303(b), 24	365, 8
303(h), 24	365(g), 9
361(1), 30	506(b), 11
361(2), 30	544(a), 38
362, 30	548, 36
362(d), 30	552(a), 9
363, 10-11, 19, 30	552(b), 9

Employee Retirement Income Security Act of 1974

SECTIONS	SECTIONS
302(c), 27	4062(d)(1)(A)(i), 28
4001(b), 27	4068(a), 27
4062(a), 27	4068(c), 27
4062(b), 27	

Tables of Authorities

Glass-Steagall Act

SECTIONS
16, 68
20, 68-69

Internal Revenue Code of 1986, as amended (Title 26, U.S.C.)

SECTIONS	SECTIONS
401, 27	860D(a)(2), 49
412(c)(11), 27	860D(a)(6), 49
412(n), 28	860E, 48
414(b), 27	860E(a), 53
414(c), 27	860E(b), 53
671, 49	860E(c), 53
672, 49	860F, 48
673, 49	860F(a), 51
674, 49	860F(b)(1)(A), 48
675, 49	860F(b)(1)(C), 49
676, 49	860G, 48
677, 49	860G(a), 51
678, 49	860G(a)(1), 49
679, 49	860G(a)(2), 49
860A, 48	860G(b), 53
860B, 48, 53	860G(c), 51
860C, 48, 53	860G(d), 51
860C(d), 53	1271(a), 52
860D, 48	1502, 26
860D(a), 51	6323, 28

Investment Company Act of 1940 (15 U.S.C. §§ 80a *et seq.*)

RULE
3a-7, 55, 58-60

Tables of Authorities

SECTIONS	SECTIONS
2(a)(36), 55	10, 54
3(a), 55	12(d), 54
3(b)(2), 58	12(e), 54
3(c)(1), 57-59	13, 55
3(c)(1)(A), 58	15(d), 55
3(c)(5), 56–57, 59	16, 54
3(c)(5)(A), 55-57	18, 54
3(c)(5)(B), 56	22, 55
3(c)(5)(C), 56	24(b), 54
3(c)(6)(A), 57	29, 55
3(c)(6)(B), 57	30, 55
3(c)(7), 58	31, 55
6(c), 58	

Securities Act of 1933 (15 U.S.C. §§ 77a *et seq.*)

RULES	RULES
144, 63	502, 62
144A, 60, 63	503, 62
415, 62	504, 62
501, 62	505, 62
501(a)(3), 63	506, 62
501(a)(5), 63	

SECTIONS	SECTIONS
3, 63	5(c), 61
3(a)(2), 63	7, 61
3(a)(3), 61, 64-65	10, 61
4(2), 61-64	

Securities Exchange Act of 1934 (15 U.S.C. §§ 78a *et seq.*)

RULE	SECTION
10b-5, 66	10(b), 66

Tables of Authorities

United States Code

29 U.S.C. § 1362(a), 27
29 U.S.C. § 1362(b), 27
29 U.S.C. § 1362(d)(1), 27
29 U.S.C. § 1368(a), 27

FEDERAL REGULATION

Code of Federal Regulations (latest edition)

12 C.F.R. pt. 3, app. A, 68
12 C.F.R. pt. 208, app. A, 68-70, 72
12 C.F.R. pt. 208, app. B, 68-70
12 C.F.R. pt. 225, app. A, 68-71, 73-76
12 C.F.R. pt. 225, app. B, 3, 68-70, 74
12 C.F.R. pt. 225, app. D, 68-70
12 C.F.R. pt. 325, app. A, 68
12 C.F.R. pt. 325, app. B, 69
12 C.F.R. pt. 567, 69
12 C.F.R. § 3.2(a), 70
26 C.F.R. pt. 1, 27
26 C.F.R. pt. 602, 27

General Counsel Memoranda

Numbers	Numbers
39,584, 47-48	37,848, 48
38,147, 48	34,602, 48

Private Letter Rulings

Numbers	Numbers
83-38-043, 47-48	79-17-085, 47
81-36-037, 47	78-48-081, 48
80-15-118, 47	78-20-017, 48
79-22-055, 47	

Tables of Authorities

Revenue Rulings

NUMBERS
92-32, 50
84-10, 48
82-144, 47
80-96, 47

NUMBERS
78-149, 50
71-399, 48
65-185, 47
54-43, 47

Treasury Regulations

SECTIONS
1.414(b), 27
1.414(c), 27
1.1502-13, 47, 50
1.1502-14, 48, 50

SECTIONS
1.1502-6, 26
301.7701-2, 51
301.7701-4(a), 50
301.7701-4(c), 50

STATE AND UNIFORM LAWS

Uniform Commercial Code

ARTICLES
1 (Louisiana), 37
3 (Louisiana), 37
4 (Louisiana), 37
5 (Louisiana), 37

ARTICLES
7 (Louisiana), 37
8 (Louisiana), 37
9 (Louisiana), 37

SECTIONS
1-103, 39
2-312, 32
2-313, 32
2-314, 32
2-315, 32
9-102, 37-38
9-102(1)(a), 39
9-105, 39
9-105(1)(b), 38
9-106, 38

SECTIONS
9-301(4), 28
9-305, 37-39
9-306(4), 40
9-308, 37
9-312, 28
9-318(1), 6
9-318(3), 40
9-318(4), 8
9-506, 32
9-506 (Delaware), 32

Index

(References are to pages.)

A

Accounting
   consolidation with originator's balance sheet, 22
   GAAP, 71-72
   requirements of REMIC, 51
   sale transactions
      definitions, 28-29
      generally, 46–47
   securitization transactions
      balance-sheet impact, 2
      generally, 35
   transfers of assets, 71-72
Accounts
   defined, 38
   generally, 37–38
   receivable loans, 65
Accredited investors, 60, 62–63
Accrual accounting, 51-53
Additional steps to protect transfer of receivables, 37-40
Adequacy of capital, guidelines for, 3
Adequate protection in bankruptcy, 11, 29–30
Adjustment of purchase price of receivables, retroactive, 32–33
Administration of collections
   duties retained by originator, 47
   generally, 33-34
Advance rates, 44-45
Advantages of securitization, 1-3
Agents
   collection, 34

Index

Agents, *continued*
    substitute collection, 42
Allied Stores Corp., 40-42
Antifraud provisions of 1934 Act, 66
Approval of securitization by bankruptcy court, 43
Arm's-length fee for collection agent, 34
Asset-backed securities risk, categories for, 76
Assets
    accounting for transfers, 71-72
    commingling, 25
    originator's consolidated with SPV's, 25-26
    transfer characterization as sale, 72
Assignment
    franchise agreements, 8-9
    trademarks, 9
    trade names, 9
Automatic stay in bankruptcy, 29–30, 43
Automobile loans, 4
Avoidance of executory contracts in bankruptcy, 8-10

B

Balance sheets
    consolidation with originator, 22
    impact of securitization, 2
Bankruptcy
    Days Inn voluntary, 10-13, 19-20
    adequate protection, 29-30
    automatic stay, 29–30, 43
    avoidance of executory contracts, 8-10
    court approval of securitization, 43
    protecting SPV from
        involuntary, 12, 16-24
        voluntary, 12, 16-24
    securitization, 40-45
    SPV as "bankruptcy-remote" entity, 23-24
Bankruptcy-remoteness, 16-27

Index

Bankrupt originators
   generally, 40-42
   securitization, 44-45
Banks
   capital requirements, 68-76
   letters of credit, 13, 15, 41, 63
   regulation, 66-76
"Blue-sky" laws, 53
Books and records, 33-34
Business
   functions commingled, 25
   trusts, 23

C

Call Report Instructions, 71-73
Capital
   contributions, 36
   requirements
      generally, 76
      risk-based, 68-76
Capital-adequacy guidelines, 3, 68-76
Capital Markets Assurance Corp. (CapMAC), 14, 44
Capital-to-risk-weighted-assets ratios, 68-70
Capital-to-total-assets ratios, 68-70
Cash collateral accounts, 15
Categories of risk
   asset-backed securities, 76
   mortgage-backed securities, 76
Characterization as
   accounting sale, 28-29, 46–47
   tax sale, 46-47
   true sale, 31-35
Charitable organizations owning SPVs, 21
Charter of SPV, 17
Chattel paper, 38
Claims, governmental, 26-27
Classes of stock in SPV, 18-19

Index

Collections
    activities SPV at risk for, 47
    administering, 33-34
    arm's-length fee for agent, 34
    commingling, 33-34, 40
    controlling, 33-34
    costs paid by originator, 34
    right to surplus, 32, 35
    substitute agents, 42
Commercial Bank Reports of Condition and Income, 71
Commercial mortgage loans, 4
Commercial-paper exemption to 1933 Act, 63-66
Commingling
    assets and business functions, 25
    collections, 33-34, 40
Common control, 26–27
Compliance with
    covenants, 28–29
    1940 Act, 58-61
    1933 Act, 61–62
Comptroller of the Currency, 66-67
Computing purchase and sale price, 6-7
Concentrated obligors risk of, 6
Consequences of failing to perfect, 37-39
Consolidated
    financial statements, 25
    tax
        groups, 26
        returns, 46–47, 50
Consolidation
    assets and liabilities of originator and SPV, 25-26
    protecting SPV from substantive, 11-12, 24-26, 43
    with originator's balance sheet (accounting), 22
Consumer loans, 65
Contractual covenants, 28–29
Contributions to capital, 36
Control
    collections, 33-34

common, 26–27
Controlled groups, 26–27
Conversion factors in credit enhancement, 73-75
Costs of collection paid by originator, 34
Court approval of securitization in bankruptcy, 43
Covenants
    compliance with, 28–29
    indenture, 3
Creating true sale of receivables, 28-35
Credit
    card receivables, 4, 41-45
    enhancement, 13-15, 41, 73-75
    establishing policy, 33
    irrevocable lines, 13
    support (third-party), 13-15, 44
Creditor of originator, SPV status as, 29
Creditors' rights, 43
Creditworthiness of third party, 14
Criteria for commercial-paper exemption to 1933 Act, 64-66
Current-transaction criterion of commercial-paper exemption, 64-66

D

Days Inn voluntary bankruptcy
    generally, 10-13, 19-20
    no-action letter, 56–57
Debtor-in-possession securitization, 40-45
Debt SPV may issue, 24
Default
    payment, 5-6
    remedies, 43
Defenses of obligors, 6
Deferring recognition of gain, 46–47
Defined-benefit pension plans, 28
Defining source of payment, 5-15
Definitions
    "account," 38
    "chattel paper," 38

Definitions, *continued*
  "investment company," 55, 58–59
  "security," 55-56
  "SPV," 1
Delay in payment, 5
Delinquent receivables, 34
Deposit accounts, 40
Determining true sale
  factors, 31-35
  generally, 43
Difficulty of segregating assets and liabilities, 25
Dilution, 43
Direct payments to SPV, 40
Directors, independent, 17, 19-20
Disclosure, 54, 61–62
Discounts and discounting
  market, 52
  original issue (OID), 52
  receivables, 6-7
  short-term acquisition, 52
Documentation refers to security for debt, 35
Duff and Phelps, 14, 44

E

Emerging Issues Task Force (EITF) requirements for SPVs, 28
Employee benefit plans, termination of, 27
English rule on perfection, 39
Enhancement of credit, 13-15
Entity-level taxation, 45, 49-51
Equipment leases, 4
Equity, *see* Substantive consolidation
Establishing credit policy, 33
Evidences of indebtedness, 55-56
Excise tax liability, 47
Executory contracts avoided in bankruptcy, 8-10
Exemption from 1940 Act
  rule 3a-7, 55, 59-61

Index

SPV petitions SEC for, 58
Extent of recourse of transferee of receivables, 31–32

F

Factors in characterization as
    tax sale, 46-47
    true sale, 31-35
Failing to perfect, consequences of, 37-39
Federal Deposit Insurance Corporation (FDIC), 71
Federal Financial Institutions Examination Council (FFIEC), 71-73
Federal Home Loan Bank Board, 3-4, 73
Federal National Mortgage Association, 3, 73
Federal Reserve System, 67-68
Fees
    attorneys', 34
    collection agents', 34
    franchising, 38
Fiduciary duties, 17, 19-20
Filing
    registration statements with SEC, 61
    UCC-1 financing statements, 37, 39
Finance charges on receivables, SPV right to, 47
Financial
    guarantees, 13-15
    institutions, 68-76
    statements consolidated, 25
Financial Guaranty Insurance Co. (FGIC), 14, 41, 44
Financial Security Assurance Inc., 14
Financing
    leases for nonpermanent capital equipment, 65
    statement (UCC-1) filed, 37, 39
FINCO structure, 21-24, 36, 47
Fitch Investors Service, Inc., 14
Fixed-income securities, 60
Franchises and franchising
    contracts, 38
    fees, 4, 57

Index

Franchises and franchising, *continued*
    generally, 7-13
Fraudulent
    conveyances
        generally, 13
        protecting against risk, 22, 35-36
    statements (liability under 1934 Act), 61–62
Future
    media revenues, 4
    payment streams, 9-13

G

GAAP, *see* Accounting
Gain recognition by originator for tax purposes, 45-49
General intangibles, 38-39
Generally accepted accounting principles (GAAP), *see* Accounting
Glass-Steagall Act, 66-68
Governmental claims, protecting SPV from, 26-27
Government National Mortgage Association, 4, 73
Grantor trust structure of SPV, 49-50
Guarantees
    financial, 13-15
    generally, 74
    parent of loans of subsidiary, 25
    springing, 20
Guidelines for adequacy of capital, 3

H

Health care receivables, 4
History of structured financing, 3-4
Holdbacks, 6-7

I

Identification of specific receivables, 46
Inadvertent investment companies, 53

Index

Incidental powers of banks, 67
Indebtedness, evidences of, 55-56
Indemnity claims, 43
Indenture covenants, 3, 28–29
Independent
   directors, 17, 19-20
   third party owning SPV, 21
   trustees, 61
Industries, regulated, 67
Institutional investors, 57, 60, 62–63
Instruments, 39
Intangibles
   "general," 38-39
   tax liability, 47
Intent of parties, 35
Interest on receivables, SPV right to, 47
Introduction to structured financing, 1-3
Inventory loans, 65
Investment company
   defined, 55, 58–59
   registration with SEC, 54-55
Investment Company Act of 1940 (1940 Act), 53-61
Investment-grade ratings, 35, 60
Investors in securities issued by SPV
   generally, 76
   tax treatment, 45, 52–53
Involuntary bankruptcy, protecting SPV from, 12, 16-24
Irrevocable credit lines, 13

J

Junk bonds, 4

L

Leases, 9-10
Legal title to receivables in SPV, 46
Legislation amending 1940 Act, 58–59

Index

Letters of credit, 13, 15, 41, 63, 74
Liability
    fraudulent statements under 1934 Act, 61–62
    omissions under 1934 Act, 61–62
    originator's consolidated with SPV's, 25-26
    tax
        excise, 47
        intangibles, 47
        SPV, 45, 49-51
Licenses, 9-10
Liens
    generally, 27
    priority over SPV, 30
Limiting
    debt SPV may issue, 24
    trade creditors SPV may have, 24
Liquidation of originator, 42–43
Liquidity, providers of, 13-15, 73-75
Loans of subsidiary guaranteed by parent, 25
Lockboxes, 40, 42
Loss recognition by originator for tax purposes, 45-49

M

Making SPV bankruptcy-remote, 16-27
Market discount, 52
Master trust, 22
Media revenues, anticipated, 4
Minimum
    capital-to-risk-weighted-assets ratios, 68-70
    capital-to-total-assets ratios, 68-70
Modifying automatic stay, 43
Moody's Investors Service, Inc., 4, 14, 41, 44
Mortgage
    loan pools (*see also* REMIC), 4, 48–49, 66–67, 73
    pass-through securities, 4
    statutes, 32
Mortgage-backed securities, risk categories for, 76

Index

Multiple classes of stock in SPV, 18-19

N

National Housing Act of 1934, 3
Nature of
    obligors, 5-7
    originator, 5-7
    receivables, 7-13
Negotiable instruments, 39
New York rule on perfection, 39
No-action letters from SEC, 56, 65–66
Nonaccredited investors, 62–63
Nonbank banks, 68
Nonrecognition of gain, 46
No-pay risk, 5-6
Notifying obligors of transfer of receivables, 33, 47

O

Obligation of originator to pay SPV costs of collection, 34
Obligor-concentration risk, 6
Obligors
    nature, 5-7
    notified of transfer, 33, 47
    statistical analysis, 5-6
Off-balance-sheet treatment, 22-23
Omissions liability under 1934 Act, 61–62
Ongoing reporting requirements under 1934 Act, 61–62
Original issue discount (OID), 52
Originator
    as prepurchase debtor of SPV, 34
    assets and liabilities consolidated with SPV, 25-26
    bankrupt, 40-45
    consolidated balance sheet for accounting purposes, 22
    liquidation of, 42–43
    nature of, 5-7
    obligated to pay SPV costs of collection, 34

Index

Originator, *continued*
    recognition of gain or loss by, 45-49
    residual interest in receivables, 46
    retained
        administrative duties, 47
        redemption right, 32
        repurchase right, 32
        servicing duties, 47
    right to surplus collections, 32, 35
    separating source of payment from, 16-45
    SPV as creditor of, 29
Overcollateralization, 6-7, 15, 21, 44
Ownership, unity of, 25

P

P.A. Bergner & Co. securitization, 44-45
Parent guarantees loans of subsidiary, 25
Parties, intent of, 35
Partnerships
    structure of SPV, 50-51
    taxation, 50
Pass-through structure of SPV transactions, 4, 45-46, 48–50, 52, 66-67
Pay-through structure of SPV transactions, 45–47, 50, 52
Payment
    default, 5-6
    defining source of, 5–15
    delay, 5
    direct to SPV, 40
    predictability, 7
    source separated from originator, 16–45
    streams, 4, 55-56
Pension
    claims against SPV, 26-27
    defined-benefit plans, 26–27
Pension Benefit Guaranty Corp. (PBGC), 27
Perfection
    English rule, 39

Index

New York rule, 39
  commingling, 34, 40
  generally, 37-40
Petition by SPV to SEC for exemption from 1940 Act, 58
Plan termination, 26-27
Pledging
  intangibles, 39
  receivables, 28
Pools of mortgage loans, *see* Mortgage loan pools
Portfolio management, 60
Possession, perfection by, 39
Predictability of payment, 5, 7
Prepurchasing debt of originator to SPV, 34
Price SPV pays for receivables
  adjusted retroactively, 32–33
  computing, 6-7
  generally, 46
Priority
  over SPV lien, 30
  PBGC, 27
Private
  investment company exemption from 1940 Act, 57
  offering
    exemption from 1933 Act, 57, 62–63
    memoranda, 63
  placement by SPV, 62–63
Private-label credit card receivables, 40-42, 44
Prohibiting speculation, 60
Promissory notes, 39
Proposed legislation amending 1940 Act, 58–59
Protecting
  against fraudulent conveyance risk, 22, 35-36
  SPV from
    governmental claims, 26-27
    involuntary bankruptcy, 12, 16-24
    substantive consolidation, 11-12, 24-26, 43
    voluntary bankruptcy, 12, 16-24
  transfer of receivables, 37-40

Index

Providers of credit enhancement or liquidity, 73-75
Public-interest exemption from 1940 Act, 58
Purchase price
   adjusted retroactively, 32–33
   computed, 6-7
Purchasing subordinated securities from SPV, 13-15

Q

Qualified institutional buyers, 60
Qualified-purchasers exemption to 1940 Act, 58–59

R

Rating agencies, 4, 14, 35, 41, 44, 60
Ratios required of Regulated Institutions, 68-70
Real estate mortgage investment conduits (REMICs), 45-46, 48–49, 51-53
Reasonable predictability of payment, 5
Receivables
   additional steps to protect transfer of, 37-40
   administration of collections of, 33-34
   as securities, 55–56
   control of collections of, 33-34
   creating true sale of, 28-35
   discounting, 6-7
   extent of recourse of transferee of, 31–32
   franchise fees, 57
   identification of specific, 46
   legal title in SPV, 46
   nature of, 7-13
   pledged, 28
   price adjusted retroactively, 32–33
   private-label credit cards, 40-42, 44
   residual interest of originator in, 46
   retained right of
      redemption, 32
      repurchase, 32

Index

SPV
   price for, 46
   rights
      defeasible, 34
      finance charges, 47
      interest, 47
   transfer reported to obligors, 47
Recognition of gain or loss by originator, 45-49
Records and books, 33-34
Recourse arrangements, 31–32, 72
Redemption, retained right of, 32
Reference to security for debt in documentation, 35
Registration
   requirements of 1933 Act, 63–64
   statement filed by SPV with SEC, 61
   with SEC as investment company, 54-55
"Regular" interests in REMIC, 48–49
Regulated industries, 66
"Regulated Institutions," 68-76
Regulation D safe-harbor provisions, 62–63
Regulatory requirements of securitization, 53-76
Remedies in default, 43
REMICs, 45-46, 48–49, 51-53
Reporting requirements under 1934 Act, 61–62
Repurchase
   agreements, 74–75
   retained right of, 32
Requirements
   ongoing reporting under 1934 Act, 61–62
   regulatory, 53-76
Reselling restricted securities, 63
Reserve accounts, 44
Residential mortgage loans and loan pools, 4, 73
Residual interests
   originator in receivables, 46
   REMIC, 48–49, 52–53
Restricted securities, 63

Index

Retail
    credit card receivables, 42
    installment paper, 65
Retained
    duties
        administrative, 47
        servicing, 47
    rights
        redemption, 32
        repurchase, 32
Retroactive adjustment of purchase price of receivables, 32–33
Rights
    redemption retained, 32
    repurchase retained, 32
    SPV
        defeasible, 34
        finance charges on receivables, 47
        interest on receivables, 47
    surplus collections, 32, 35
Risk
    categories
        asset-backed securities, 76
        mortgage-backed securities, 76
    concentrated obligors, 6
    transferred for collection activities, 47
Risk-based capital requirements, 3, 68-76
Rule 3a-7 under 1940 Act, 55, 59-61
Rule 10b-5 under 1934 Act, 66
Rule 144 under 1933 Act, 63
Rule 144A under 1933 Act, 63

S

Safe-harbor provisions of SEC regulation D, 62–63
Sale
    assets (characterization as), 72
    price computed, 6-7
    "true," *see* True sale

Index

Savings and loan associations, 3-4
"Section 20 subsidiaries" of banks, 68
Securities
    issued by SPV
        not exempt under 1933 Act section 3(a)(3), 61
        tax treatment of investors in, 45, 52-53
    restricted, 63
Securities Act of 1933 (1933 Act)
    accredited investors, 60
    generally, 53, 61-66
    institutional investors, 60
Securities and Exchange Commission (SEC)
    accounting requirements for SPVs, 28
    exemption from 1940 Act, 58
    investment company registration, 54-55
    no-action letters, 56, 65–66
    registration statements, 61
    regulation D safe-harbor provisions, 62–63
Securities Exchange Act of 1934 (1934 Act), 54, 61-66
Securities Industry Association, 67-68
Securitization (*see also* Structured financing)
    advantages, 1-3
    approved by bankruptcy court, 43
    balance-sheet impact, 2
    bankrupt originators, 44-45
    bankruptcy, 40-45
    private-label credit card receivables, 40-42
    regulatory requirements, 53-76
    tax issues, 46-53
Security
    defined, 55-56
    referred to in documentation, 35
Segregating
    assets and liabilities (difficulty), 25
    collections, 34
Senior/subordinate structures, 13
Separating source of payment from originator, 16-45
Servicing duties retained by originator, 47

Index

Short-term
   acquisition discount, 52
   commercial loans, 65
"Slow-pay" risk, 5
Source of payment
   defining, 5-15
   separated from originator, 16-45
Special-purpose vehicle (SPV)
   defined, 1
   assets and liabilities consolidated with originator, 25-26
   at risk for collection activities, 47
   bankruptcy-exempt entity, 23-24
   bankruptcy-remote, 16-27
   charter of, 17
   collection costs paid by originator, 34
   conditions on 1940 Act exemption, 59-61
   creditor of originator, 29
   direct payments to, 40
   filing registration statement with SEC, 61-62
   grantor trust structure of, 49–50
   legal title to receivables in, 46
   lien with priority over, 30
   limitations on
      debt, 24
      trade creditors, 24
   multiple classes of stock in, 18-19
   owned by independent third party, 21
   partnership structure, 50-51
   pass-through transaction structure, 4, 45–46, 48–50, 52, 66–67
   pay-through transaction structure, 45–47, 50, 52
   pension claims against, 26-27
   petitioning SEC for exemption from 1940 Act, 58
   prepurchase creditor of originator, 34
   price for receivables, 46
   private placement by, 62–63
   protected from
      governmental claims, 26-27
      involuntary bankruptcy, 12, 16-24

Index

    substantive consolidation, 11-12, 24-26, 43
    voluntary bankruptcy, 12, 16-24
  purchase of subordinated securities from, 13-15
  REMIC transaction structure, 45–46, 48–49, 51–53
  rights
    defeasible, 34
    finance charges on receivables, 47
    interest on receivables, 47
  securities exemption under 1933 Act section 3(a)(3), 61
  structured as trust, 23
  tax
    claims against, 26
    liability, 45, 49-51
    treatment of investors in securities issued by, 45, 52-53
Specific receivables, identification of, 46
Speculation prohibited, 60
Springing guarantees, 20
Standard & Poor's Corp., 4, 14, 41, 44
State
  "blue-sky" laws, 53
  excise tax liability, 47
  intangibles tax liability, 47
  mortgage statutes, 32
Statement of Financial Accounting Standards No. 77, 28, 71-72
Statistical analysis of obligors, 5-6
Stays in bankruptcy, automatic, 29, 43
Steps to protect transfer of receivables, 37-40
Stock in SPV, multiple classes of, 18-19
Streams of payments, 4
Structured financing (*see also* Securitization)
  exempted from 1940 Act by rule 3a-7, 55, 59-61
  history of, 3-4
  introduction to, 1-3
  investors in, 76
  nature of
    obligors in, 5-7
    originator in, 5-7

Index

Structure of SPV
   corporation, 17-19, 51
   grantor trust, 49–50
   partnership, 50-51
   trust, 23, 49–50
   two-tiered, 21-24
Subordinated securities purchased from SPV, 13-15
Subordination, 50, 72
Subrogation, 4, 14
Subsidiary loans guaranteed by parent, 25
Substantive consolidation, protecting SPV from, 11-12, 24-26, 43
Substitute collection agents, 42
Surety bonds, 13-14
Surplus collections, right to, 32, 35
Sweeping funds from originator's deposit accounts and lockboxes, 40

T

Tax and taxation
   claims against SPV, 26
   issues in securitization, 45-53
   liability of SPV, 45, 49-51
   loan transactions, 47
   partnerships, 50-51
   returns, 35
   sale
      characterization as, 47
      generally, 46–47
   treatment of investors in securities issued by SPV, 45, 52-53
Termination of employee benefit plans, 26-27
Third-party
   credit support, 13-15, 44
   ownership of SPV, 21
Title to receivables in SPV, 46
Trade
   creditors SPV may have limited, 24
   names, 21

Index

receivables
    exception to 1940 Act, 56-57
    generally, 4, 7, 42
Trademarks, 21
Transferee of receivables, extent of recourse of, 31–32
Transfer of
   assets (accounting for), 71-72
   receivables
     additional steps to protect, 37-40
     reported to obligors, 47
True sale
   created, 28-35
   determining
     factors, 31-35
     generally, 43
   generally, 7, 41
Trustees independent, 61
Trust, SPV structured as, 23, 49-50
Two-tiered structure, 21-24, 36, 47

U

UCC-1 financing statement filed, 37, 39
Uncollectible receivables, 34
Underpricing receivables, 6
Underwriting prohibited by Glass-Steagall Act, 66–67
Unity of ownership, 25

V

Voluntary bankruptcy
   Days Inn, 10-13, 19-20
   protecting SPV from, 12, 16-24

New Second Edition...

Structured Finance
A Guide to the Principles of Asset Securitization
By Steven L. Schwarcz
(Kaye, Scholer, Fierman, Hays & Handler, New York City)

Ordering Information:

To order additional copies of this indispensable reference work, call (212) 765-5700 or write Department SAB3 (or you may use the Order Form on the reverse of the next page), Practising Law Institute, 810 Seventh Avenue, New York, NY 10019.
The price per single copy is $29.95...

Order three or more copies and save at least 15%!

Also recommended and available on 30-day approval

A step-by-step, how-to-approach with this new Second Edition . . .

Asset-Based Lending
A Practical Guide to Secured Financing
By Peter H. Weil
(Kaye, Scholer, Fierman, Hays & Handler, New York City)

You'll want this book on your desk when these questions come up in your practice . . .

- What is the best way to make loans secured by receivables?
- What is factoring?
- What are the benefits of debt and lien subordination?
- How should you structure a loan participation?
- What effect does the borrower's bankruptcy have on an asset-based loan?
- What is the function of covenants in a secured loan?
- How can you minimize the risk of lawsuits for lender liability?

December 1992, $115, PLI Order #A1-1416 (hardcover)

Call or write for detailed brochure!

*To order your approval copies,
complete and mail the order form on the next page!*

Customer Order Information:

PLI Publications are sold on 30-day approval, and may be returned for a full refund or credit

Sales Tax: California and Illinois residents please add applicable sales tax to price of publications

Prices subject to change without notice

Shipping and Handling Charges: If check accompanies order, PLI will absorb UPS shipping and handling charges in the United States, U.S. possessions, and Canada. *Credit Card orders and orders to be billed are subject to a $7 minimum regular UPS shipping and handling charge.* PLI waives this charge for PLI Associate Members. UPS requires a street address.

THREE DIFFERENT WAYS TO ORDER

MAIL:
Complete the order form and mail it to:
PRACTISING LAW INSTITUTE,
810 Seventh Avenue, New York, N.Y. 10019

PHONE:
CALL [212] 765-5710
Source Code: SAB3

FAX 3:
1[800] 321-0093

☐ A1-1418 Structured Finance (Second Edition), $29.95
☐ A1-1416 Asset-Based Lending: A Practical Guide to Secured Financing, $115

☐ Future new editions
☐ Future supplements and/or new editions

$ _____ check enclosed.   ☐ Bill my firm   ☐ Bill me
(Payable to Practising Law Institute)

Please Charge to: ☐ Visa ☐ MasterCard ☐ American Express

Credit Card No.: _____ Exp. Date: _____

Signature: _____
(signature required on all credit card orders)

PLEASE PRINT IN BOXES. USE CAPITAL LETTERS. SPACE BETWEEN WORDS.

FIRST NAME | INITIAL | LAST NAME

FIRST NAME | INITIAL | LAST NAME

FIRM NAME (First Three Names Are Sufficient)

STREET ADDRESS (Use Street Address For UPS Delivery – Not P.O. Box Number)

SUITE NO., FLOOR, ETC.

CITY | STATE | ZIP CODE | AREA | PHONE NUMBER

SAB3